Public Relations as a Creative Industry

This shortform book defines and situates the role of Public Relations as a creative industry and discusses the trends and issues that the sector is facing within the wider context of the Creative Industries.

Traversing and distilling both industry and scholarly research, the author will call on perspectives from a range of areas, including creativity, psychology, advertising, and marketing. Creativity and innovation are crucial elements in times of profound transformation such as those being experienced nowadays by the PR industry. The ability to generate new ideas is a competitive advantage of organizations. Nevertheless, although traditionally the focus has been on individual creativity, this book highlights the importance of organizational creativity in PR, becoming a result of teamwork and social interaction.

This book will be a valuable resource for researchers and scholars looking at how creativity is an important asset in Public Relations. It will also be useful for students of Corporate Communication and Public Relations studies, for both undergraduate and postgraduate programs and PR practitioners who want to increase their creativity, learning from creative techniques and case studies.

Elisenda Estanyol is Lecturer in Information and Communication Studies at Universitat Oberta de Catalunya (UOC), Spain.

Routledge Research in the Creative and Cultural Industries
Series Editor: Ruth Rentschler

This series brings together book-length original research in cultural and creative industries from a range of perspectives. Charting developments in contemporary cultural and creative industries thinking around the world, the series aims to shape the research agenda to reflect the expanding significance of the creative sector in a globalised world.

Music as Labour
Inequalities and Activism in the Past and Present
Edited by Dagmar Abfalter and Rosa Reitsamer

Risk in the Film Business
Known Unknowns
Michael Franklin

Orchestra Management
Models and Repertoires for the Symphony Orchestra
Arne Herman

The Venice Arsenal
Between History, Heritage, and Re-use
Edited by Luca Zan

Managing Cultural Joint Ventures
An Identity-Image View
Tanja Johansson, Annukka Jyrämä and Kaari Kiitsak-Prikk

Public Relations as a Creative Industry
Elisenda Estanyol

For more information about this series, please visit: www.routledge.com/ Routledge-Research-in-the-Creative-and-Cultural-Industries/book-series/RRCCI

Public Relations as a Creative Industry

Elisenda Estanyol

Routledge
Taylor & Francis Group

LONDON AND NEW YORK

First published 2023
by Routledge
4 Park Square, Milton Park, Abingdon, Oxon OX14 4RN

and by Routledge
605 Third Avenue, New York, NY 10158

Routledge is an imprint of the Taylor & Francis Group, an informa business

British Library Cataloguing-in-Publication Data
A catalogue record for this book is available from the British Library

Library of Congress Cataloging-in-Publication Data
Names: Estanyol Casals, Elisenda, author.
Title: Public relations as a creative industry / Elisenda Estanyol.
Description: Abingdon, Oxon ; New York, NY : Routledge, 2023. |
   Series: Routledge research in the creative and cultural industries |
   Includes bibliographical references and index.
Identifiers: LCCN 2022023818 (print) | LCCN 2022023819 (ebook) |
   ISBN 9781032160481 (hardback) | ISBN 9781032160498 (paperback) |
   ISBN 9781003246879 (ebook)
Subjects: LCSH: Public relations. | Cultural industries. |
   Creative ability.
Classification: LCC HD59 .E88 2023 (print) |
   LCC HD59 (ebook) | DDC 659.2—dc23/eng/20220526
LC record available at https://lccn.loc.gov/2022023818
LC ebook record available at https://lccn.loc.gov/2022023819

ISBN: 978-1-032-16048-1 (hbk)
ISBN: 978-1-032-16049-8 (pbk)
ISBN: 978-1-003-24687-9 (ebk)

DOI: 10.4324/9781003246879

Typeset in Times New Roman
by Apex CoVantage, LLC

Contents

1 Introduction and literature review/context

1.1 Introduction

Creativity is an exciting and complex object of study, which has received little attention at a scientific level from the discipline of public relations (PR). The objective of this book is to describe the role that creativity currently plays in the PR industry, studying how it is managed within organizations and the practitioners who work in it. Moreover, creativity methods that can be applied when planning and executing PR projects, programs, and actions, will be proposed.

1.2 Public relations: a creative industry that adapts to changing contexts

Institutions and public and private companies are becoming increasingly more aware of the importance of communicating with their stakeholders (customers, employees, shareholders, suppliers, government institutions, etc.) using different techniques and means, which are also rapidly increasing thanks to new technologies and the new context of digital communication, with the proliferation of social media and mobile applications. This proliferation of new channels facilitates the dissemination of messages and favors more personalization, but, at the same time, there is less control of these by the sender. Audiences are becoming increasingly fragmented, their attention span has decreased, and there is the risk of saturation.

In this new context, the notoriety and differentiation of messages end up becoming decisive factors for their effectiveness. Creativity can help make these messages more relevant to target audiences and make them more memorable. Creativity, understood as the ability to generate new, unique, and appropriate ideas, can help find solutions to communication problems

DOI: 10.4324/9781003246879-1

in organizations. Drawing from these considerations, the following is proposed as a **definition of creativity in PR:**

> *Creativity in public relations is the process that makes it possible to find alternative and typically unconventional solutions, which can improve relations and communication between an organization and its publics.*

Beyond the technological changes, there are multiple factors that affect how organizations communicate with their audiences. The continuous sociocultural changes, the globalization of the economy, the technological transformation, the surge in fake news, climate change, and the supervening crises (like the COVID-19 pandemic) are also elements that impact the PR industry, and consequently, the way in which communication plans are developed and carried out, requiring additional creativity be applied.

Beyond its instrumental value for business, the credibility and creativity of PR programs have a strong strategic component for the generation, maintenance, or change of attitudes among the population. This becomes a key factor in the current context with the emergence of antiscience movements (climate change deniers, vaccine skeptics, etc.), fake news, and popular disinformation campaigns.

Creativity has become an asset in the business world, a crucial element for business in a competitive environment. From the industrial society, we have moved on to the information and communication society, described by Castells (2004), in which technology plays a key role. In this new environment, markets are dynamic and force organizations to constantly adapt. As pointed out already by Golen in 1983, creativity is a necessity in business, since it is often required to find unique solutions to existing problems. De Bono (1995) warns that in a highly competitive industry "doing it better is not enough, it must be done differently" (p. 51). Based on this reflection and others, trends in marketing have emerged, such as lateral marketing, developed by Kotler and Trías De Bes (2003), which aims to apply innovation not just into inventing new products, but also into the development of new processes, new channels, and new business concepts.

Most of the academic literature about creativity in the business world views creativity as a competitive advantage for organizations. However, it basically focuses on the attributes that the employees in the organization must have, without putting the same emphasis into creating an organizational environment that favors and nurtures creativity. In this regard, Mumford and Gustafson (1988) warn that even when individuals have developed their creative capacity, the willingness to utilize their creative efforts within the organization will be conditioned by the beliefs about the consequences that this may cause them. Therefore, the fact that a company has creative people will not be enough if it does not know how to stimulate and recognize this potential. The PR industry should be focusing then on fostering the creative talent of its professionals, while at the same time, creating a favorable environment to stimulate creativity.

1.3 Creativity as a professional skill of the PR practitioner

Creativity is one of the most important qualities that a professional should possess. For CEOs, creativity continues to be a highly valued skill when it comes to adding new talent into their teams, given the fact that it is impossible to replace human talent with machines. In fact, in PwC's 20th CEO survey (PwC, 2022), 77% of CEOs indicated that problem-solving skills, creativity, and innovation were soft skills in high demand. Other recent studies, like the *Global Talent Trends* conducted by LinkedIn (Dey, 2021), highlight that creativity ranks first among the soft skills most in demand by companies today. It is followed by the ability to deal with complexity and ambiguity, and Communication. Indeed, creativity is an aspect of human capital that is very valuable in companies, since it cannot be generated in a factory, but rather, is created by the individuals themselves by applying abstract thought.

If we look at the PR industry, we also see how creativity comes in second place among the relevant skill sets for future talent, according to the study by the International Communications Consultancy Organisation (ICCO) (2020), just behind Data, measurement, and analytics. The European Communication Monitor (EUPRERA, 2021a) includes creativity within the competencies for acting as a communicator, which it defines as the ability to develop communication strategies, create content, and build relationships.

There are many authors as well who, from the PR field, exhort the sector to stimulate creativity. As such, Wilcox et al. (2012) identify among the essential skills that a PR professional should possess (1) writing skill; (2) research ability; (3) planning expertise; (4) problem-solving ability; and (5) business and economics competence. It is precisely in skill 4 (ability to solve problems), where they mention creativity, noting that "innovative ideas and fresh approaches are needed to solve complex problems or to make a public relations program unique and memorable" (p. 34). Cutlip et al. (2000) also mention the ability to solve problems, curiosity, and frustration tolerance among some of the qualities that a PR professional should have. Likewise, Pieczka and L'Etang (2006) highlight the importance of creativity and mental flexibility in PR practitioners, noting that their "focus on personal qualities such as creativity, lateral thinking, flexibility, articulateness, persuasiveness, common sense, and integrity is important" (p. 276). In this sense, Green (2009) emphasizes that creativity is a vital skill in the PR profession, yet most people in the industry have not received any training in this area. Other authors like Hallahan (1999), Daymon (2001), Leichliter (2001), Austin (2007), Gregory (2008), and Palea (2010) agree that developing creative solutions is part of the PR planning process and that it is a skill, therefore, that must be cultivated by the industry itself. But what exactly is creativity and how can it be stimulated? We will see next that Psychology has been the discipline that has addressed this issue the most and how PR can adopt some of its postulates.

1.4 Psychology of creativity

Even if there seems to be a certain consensus on the importance of developing creativity skill among PR professionals, we need to delve deeper into what it means to be creative, how the creative process is developed, and how creativity can be encouraged.

Creativity still tends to be associated in part of the collective imagination with inspiration and a gift that only some individuals possess, as if they had been touched by a magic wand. The belief still exists that it is an innate quality and that creative individuals are inspired geniuses who have an intuition that cannot be explained or taught. Creativity, understood from this point of view, is shrouded in an air of mystery.

Scientific research and nondeterministic theories have made it possible to demystify this vision of creativity, and, to date, most experts understand creativity as a capacity that can be developed by people and, consequently, can be practiced and taught.

Psychologists, sociologists, philosophers, anthropologists, historians, and communicators have tried to decipher the characteristics of creativity over the years, giving rise to different theories and multiple definitions of creativity. Up to the point that in 1959, Taylor had already compiled more than a hundred definitions of what creativity is.

Psychology, and mainly Cognitive Psychology, has been the discipline that has carried out the most exhaustive research on creativity, giving it a scientific character through theoretical and experimental research. In fact, many of its postulates have later been incorporated into the theories of creativity formulated from other disciplines. From the psychology standpoint, creativity simultaneously refers to a cognitive process and the result of this process (the product or creative idea), to an attribute of the individual and to an environment (Rhodes, 1961). Notable scientific theories on creativity include The Associative Creativity Theory (Mednick, 1962), The Conceptual Spaces Theory (Boden, 1996), The Theory of Multiple Intelligences (Gardner, 2004), The Investment Theory of Creativity (Sternberg, 2006), and The Concept of Flow (Csikszentmihalyi, 2015).

Initially, those researching creativity focused on the study of the creative individual (their characteristics, their personality, etc.), to later change course and stop focusing on studying the person as an isolated entity, in order to examine how they interact with the environment. The contributions of Amabile (1983) stand out in this approach.

Thus, while in the 19th century the predominant belief was that only artists (painters, sculptors, musicians, photographers, film directors, etc.) were creative, during the 20th century, creative expression started to apply to all areas of culture, science, and ultimately to everything that is the result of human production. The most commonly accepted definition of creativity is the ability to produce an idea or product that is new and valuable. This is why, nowadays, the use of the word creativity basically refers to the process that takes place in the mind of a creator, regardless of the field and, therefore, also in the professional practice of PR.

The beginning of research on creativity in a disciplinary way is usually situated around the year 1950, when the president of the American Psychological Association (APA), Joy Paul Guilford, held the "Creativity" conference (Guilford, 1950), where he evidenced the little research that had been carried out on the subject up until that point. Guilford defined creativity as the skills that are characteristic of creative individuals, such as fluency, flexibility, originality, and divergent thinking (concepts we will explore further in Chapter 2). Guilford's work acted as a catalyst to spark the interest of the scientific community in the study of creativity.

Guilford distinguished productive thinking into two classes: *convergent thinking*, which is based on already known ideas and content and requires finding the one valid answer; and *divergent thinking*, which explores different directions and generates a variety and quantity of information in order to find the best solution or several appropriate solutions. Divergent thinking is characterized by *originality, fluency*, and *flexibility*. According to this author, creativity is the result of divergent thinking and would be directly related to the ability to connect and relate apparently divergent ideas, that is, to find similarities where, by default, none seem to exist. This is the type of thinking related to creativity that later inspired Edward De Bono (1995) to formulate his proposal on the concept of lateral thinking.

After the Guilford conference, the study of creativity experienced a strong boost and centers and initiatives dedicated to its research were created, with important theorists at the forefront, among them were the Aptitude Research Project, directed by Guilford; the Institute for Personality Research and Assessment, with Frank Barron; the Pedagogical Institute of the University of Minnesota, with Ellis Paul Torrance; the Utah Conferences, with Irving A. Taylor and Brewster Ghiselin; the Richardson Foundation, of the APA; and the Alex F. Osborn's Creative Education Foundation, with Alex F.

Osborn and William J. J. Gordon. Years later, the first specialized scientific publications would also appear, such as the *Journal of Creative Behaviour* (created in 1967) and the *Creativity Research Journal* (created in 1988).

Creativity quickly came to be considered one of the components of intelligence, being studied by authors such as Howard Gardner, Joy Paul Guilford, and Robert J. Sternberg. Sternberg, who was also the president of the APA, summarized in an article published in 2006 his theory of creativity (The Investment Theory of Creativity), which is included in the Theory of Intelligence, by the same author, according to which the intelligence of individuals is based on their creative, analytical, and practical abilities. According to this author, creativity depends on the interrelation between intellectual abilities, knowledge, styles of thinking, personality, motivation, and environment.

1.5 Definition of public relations

If, as L'Etang (2009) points out, we understand the discipline of PR not only as a part of the management of organizations, but as a dynamic and flexible discipline, geared toward solving problems and integrated in the complex postindustrial societies and in a wide range of contexts: political, scientific, health, etc.; both creativity and PR become transversal processes that permeate a large part of society.

Most of the definitions of PR coincide in viewing PR as the management of communication to establish good relations and mutual understanding between an organization and its publics. In 1984, Grunig and Hunt highlighted the importance of the concept of *relation* between organizations (whether they are private companies, associations, or public entities) and all their publics (not only consumers, but also employees, investors, suppliers, the media, etc.)

The scientific definition of PR has evolved, emphasizing the importance for these relationships to be "mutually beneficial", that is, that they add value to both organizations and their publics. For example, Cutlip et al. (2000) define PR as the managerial function that identifies, establishes, and maintains mutually beneficial relationships between an organization and the different publics on which its successes and failures depend.

Dozier and Lauzen (2000) proposed a definition of PR seen as a scientific discipline, beyond a professional activity, describing it as "the study of action, communication, and relationships between organizations and publics, as well as the study of the intended and unintended consequences of those relationships for individuals and society as a whole" (p. 4).

PR is a relatively recent professional practice, which caused it to have to define its own identity, often trying to define its functions by differentiating them from other practices such as advertising or marketing. Thus, it is not surprising that different professional associations in the sector have contributed to its definition. For example, the Public Relations Society of America (PRSA), an association that brings together professionals in the sector in the United States, launched a campaign in 2012 to redefine professional activity itself. After months of proposals and votes, the result was the following "Public relations is a strategic communication process that builds mutually beneficial relationships between organizations and their publics" (PRSA, 2012).

1.6 Public relations and its societal roles

Traditionally, PR have been studied from a functional perspective, from the strategic management paradigm and the Theory of Excellence formulated by University of Maryland professor, James E. Grunig, in his book *Excellence in Public Relations and Communication Management* (1992). Grunig defended the strategist role of the PR professional within organizations, since they help with communication actions to achieve the goals and vision of the organization. In 1984, Grunig and Hunt established a classification of four PR models:

(1) the *press agent model*: In this model, PR performs a persuasive function through one-way communication from the organization to the publics;

(2) the *public information model*: In this model, PR aims to disseminate information to one or more publics, and it is not necessary to do so in a persuasive way. It is a one-way model, from sender to receiver, in which the truth does matter;

(3) the *two-way asymmetrical model*: It aims to scientifically persuade the publics. In this model, PR uses methods and techniques from the social sciences to study the behaviors and attitudes of the publics, with the aim that they accept the organization's point of view. Communication is two-way, from sender to receiver, and from receiver back to sender, but the power resides with the sender, whose intent is to persuade the receiver to accept or support the organization;

(4) the *two-way symmetrical model*: It is based on the dialogue between the organization and the public. In this model, both parties are able to be persuaded to change their attitudes or behaviors as a result of the PR activity. For Grunig and Hunt, this last model is the one that represents excellence in PR.

This prevailing theory in PR began to be questioned a few decades ago for being considered too functional and at the service of companies and institutions, with the emergence of new approaches and theories, such as the Critical Paradigm; the Rhetorical Paradigm; the Feminist Paradigm; or Dialogic Theory. These paradigms consider that the dominant theory has focused on the study of the effectiveness, evaluation, professionalism, role, and status of PR, forgetting other important issues such as language, persuasion, rhetoric (Heath, 2006), and dialogue (Kent & Taylor, 2002). They are approaches that strive to offer a sociological perspective that aims to go beyond organizational communication and that includes in its study other entities such as nations, institutions, communities, and non-profit organizations (Xifra, 2017). *Como apuntan* Moloney and McGrath (2019) "PR must be considered as rhetoric as it will most always fall under public scrutiny in a marketplace of differing ideas and points-of-view and must be persuasive to make itself seen and heard" (Auger, 2021, p. 222).

Authors such as Heath (2006), McKie and Munshi (2007), Coombs and Holladay (2007), Ihlen and Van Ruler (2009), L'Etang (2009), and Edwards and Hodges (2016) began to approach the discipline by focusing on its influence in society. *Sriramesh and Verčič (2007) also point out that PR is often erroneously perceived as only involving corporate activities, and that the specialized academic literature has not focused enough* "on the use of public relations for altruistic and information campaigns" (p. 355). It is for that reason that, next, we will see how PR can be examined from different levels: **micro**, **meso**, and **macro**, which helps to offer a more holistic view of the profession.

1.6.1 Micro level

From this micro level, the PR profession focuses on providing services to organizations, from a basically functional approach, although it has evolved over the years. Since the 1950s, when the practice was mainly focused on media relations and publicity (the disclosure of information by a company, an entity, or a public body in order to create a favorable climate for it which is disseminated through the media, creating a free space); until today, in which multiple and diverse areas of specialization are developed and there are different models of professionalization.

From this level, PR is studied from a more operational and technical function. As described by Grunig and Hunt (1984) and Sha (2007), the operational dimension is associated with the technical activities and tactics responsible for disseminating communication through the execution of certain tasks. The tactical dimension involves the way PR strategies are executed.

Creativity is very useful at the micro level, as it allows us to think of new and original ways of executing PR plans, from the design of an event to launch a new product, to the format and content of a press kit to send to the media, the storytelling of a campaign, or the photographs and messages shared by the organization through social media.

1.6.2 Meso level

Although creativity is often associated with the tactical level of PR, it is equally necessary at the strategic, meso, and macro levels.

From the perspective of the meso level, PR are conducted as an essential activity for the proper functioning of the organization and, in it, the professional becomes a communication strategist and participates in decision making that concerns all the issues that may arise. impact the organization. At this level, it contributes to defining the purpose of the organization, its mission, vision, and values, and the strategy is designed to communicate them and establish links with the public.

As Ferrari (2013, p. 13–14) points out, in their strategic role, the PR professional is responsible for:

(a) integrating the "dominant coalition" (the top management of the organization), participating in decision making, guiding, and offering recommendations on the execution of policies, guidelines, and communication plans;

(b) conceiving and formulating the overall planning of public relations, associating it with the major objectives of the company and the policies and guidelines of the organization;

(c) establishing mechanisms for measuring the results and indicating the cost-benefit ratio of the communication effort as a process that adds value to business;

(d) assuming the management of relations with the public of interest, also acting as a defender of the "voices" of the public through negotiation, mediation, and consensus;

(e) being adequately prepared to assume the role of consultant to the organization's senior management and to represent it before government agencies, entities, and institutions of interest to the organization, to deal with issues related to the communicational context and its reputation;

(f) assuming the management of corporate communication in all its dimensions, from the strengthening of the elements that make up the identity, which entails respecting the values of culture, ethics, and the guidelines and policies of the organization.

1.6.3 Macro level

In addition to helping organizations, PR can be studied from a macro level to understand how they contribute to society. From this perspective, PR can contribute to raising awareness about issues such as climate change, human rights, and gender equality, and influence the construction of national identities and the consolidation of democracy (Yang & Taylor, 2013). Other authors like Edwards (2018) have also studied the social significance of PR, stating that "the effects of public relations work must be measured in social and cultural terms, as well as in terms of organizational interests" (p. 5).

Authors like Moloney and McGrath (2019) argue that the role of PR in society should advocacy and counter-advocacy and that PR has a role and effect on the political economy and the society.

The Fully Functioning Society Theory (FFST) is a PR theory formulated by Heath (2006, 2018) that argues that for organizations to be successful they need to contribute to society. Toth (2010, p. 717) summarizes the eight premises of this theory:

(1) management of organizations must demonstrate the characteristics that fosters legitimacy;
(2) organizational legitimacy is based on sound principle of corporate responsibility;
(3) management must be able to assess whether power is used for only narrow interests or the larger interests of society;
(4) self-interests are an irrefutable part of the human experience;
(5) relationships are symmetrical when they reflect the good of the whole community;
(6) society is a complex of collectives engaged in variously constructive dialogues;
(7) public discourses must make available evidence, facts, identifications, and policy choices;
(8) in addition to advocacy, rhetors may lead us to enlightened choices through shared narratives and identifications.

From this point of view/premise, PR can be adopted by activists and social movement organizations (SMOs) to defend very diverse causes. Some of the traditional tactics of activism are demonstrations and protest actions, which contribute to increasing awareness.

A growth in activism is predicted in the coming years as a result of a lack of faith in government and an increase in political polarization, as well as a greater commitment from companies when it comes to positioning themselves on societal issues (USC Annenberg Center for Public Relations & Global Alliance for Public Relations and Communication Management, 2021).

Box 1.1   PR and climate change

PR can help through communication to raise awareness in society and companies about climate change, creating an orientation on the possible solutions that can be taken in terms of sustainable development. McKie and Galloway (2007) and Almiron and Xifra (2019) are some of the authors who have addressed climate change denial and how it can be reinforced or, on the contrary, combated by PR, depending on the interests of the promoting subject (be it an organization or a social movement). In this sense, there are large corporations and lobbies that promote inaction in the face of climate change, while other companies, governments, NGOs, and activist movements fight to raise public awareness and apply real measures to combat it.

Box 1.2   PR and gender equality

On March 7, 2022, Mexico City woke up with a zeppelin flying over its sky. On its sides, you could read **"10 femicides a day"**. Images of the action were broadcast the next day on many televisions around the world, coinciding with International Women's Day. The action was organized by Fuimos Todas, a women's group that seeks to make violence against women in Mexico visible (Miranda, 2022).

Another example is the **Me Too** movement, which made a great worldwide impact, also thanks to the application of PR techniques and tactics in its dissemination. Originally this movement was created in 2006 on Myspace by the African–American activist Tarana Burke to encourage the empowerment of black women. However, the explosion of the #MeToo viral phenomenon occurred in 2017 when thousands of women began to use this hashtag to report their experiences of sexual harassment on social media. As pointed out by *Saavedra (2019)*,

> *the first reports came out in the American film industry, which made it possible for a feminist demand – the fight against sexual harassment – to reach a level of international visibility, relevance and social influence that had not been seen in years (p. 182).*

As described by Xiong et al. (2019), the #MeToo movement promoted the mobilization online:

> using hashtags facilitates the diagnostic behaviors in social movements – online users frequently referred to related issues

(e.g., whom should be blamed) that mobilized the movement. Hashtags were also used for the purposes of promoting local events, identifying leading activists, and initiating actions in online activism (p. 20).

Aside from Me Too, the contribution of PR to feminism, understood as the social movement that seeks to end discrimination on the basis of gender, has been addressed by authors such as Fitch (2016) and Fitch et al. (2016), among others.

Box 1.3   PR and human rights

As described by Wilcox et al. (2012), in the mid-1960s, the civil rights movement in the United States, led by its leader Martin Luther King, effectively used PR techniques and tactics such as organizing events, lobbying, and giving speeches to achieve their goals.

More recently, after the death of George Floyd at the hands of the US police in 2020, and the cell phone recording of the event being spread on social media, the **Black Lives Matter** movement was born. This movement achieved a wide international repercussion, and numerous adhesions, to the point that companies that had never applied for social causes expressed their support for this cause against police abuse and racism (USC Annenberg Center for Public Relations & Global Alliance for Public Relations and Communication Management, 2021).

1.7 The public relations industry

PR is a creative industry that adapts to establish the best way to relate an organization with its stakeholders. To do this, today it has multiple channels (many already digital), which allow much more personalized communication, and also thanks to big data.

However, the practice of PR dates back to the earliest civilizations. Rhetoric, political communication, campaigns to influence public opinion, etc. They were already very present in Greek and Roman societies, for example, and there were professionals who dedicated themselves to their practice. Even so, the origin of the PR industry has traditionally been located in the Anglo-Saxon countries in the middle of the last century, as it was when the first PR firms emerged and their contribution to the economy of the countries began to be calculated. The PR industry also flourished later in those countries with higher economic activity and thanks to the expansion of democracy after World War II, until today, with PR representing an important economic activity in North America, Central America, South America, Asia, Oceania, and Europe. *The weight* of the industry in Africa, although not yet as representative, shows a growth rate that is also important (Sriramesh &Verčič, 2019). If we look at their growth, the top 250 PR firms reported fee income of around $13.2bn in 2020 (PRovoke, 2021), when this figure was $7bn in 2007 (The Holmes Report, 2007).

Thus, in recent decades, globalization has had an impact on the development of PR, while PR have also contributed to the spread of globalization (Sriramesh & Verčič, 2007). This presents a challenge for the theory of PR (Elmer, 2007, and also for education and for the profession itself (Sriramesh, 2010), which should be able to offer a multicultural approach to the way communication programs are developed, helping to build relationships with local cultures; collaborate in solving shared problems in a globalized world, such as climate change, poverty, or pandemics (Wakefield, 2010). As pointed out by Taylor (2000) "successful organizations must understand the intercultural and international aspects of public relations" (p. 277), so when it comes to designing and executing communication plans, the national and regional peculiarities at an economic, social, and cultural level must be taken into account.

Recently, the impact of COVID-19 has caused significant impacts on the economy and, consequently, PR industry as well, which saw its growth decline in 2021 for the first time in the last decade (4%, according to PRovoke, 2021). Nonetheless, the PRCA census 2021 prepared by the Public Relations and Communications Association (PRCA) shows that the industry is coming out of the crisis, gradually resuming the activity that was suspended or reduced during the pandemic. For its part, the report by PRovoke (2021) also shows how, during the pandemic, although investments in event organization and marketing communication were reduced, other areas were reinforced, such as crisis communication, internal communication, and public affairs, while there was an increase in the demand for communication services in sectors such as healthcare and B2B technology.

During the pandemic, creativity also become a key value for the PR industry. This is evidenced by the *Creativity in PR 2021 Global Study*, conducted by PRovoke Media and Now Go Create, in partnership with FleishmanHillard. The majority of the participants in the study (more than 300 agency and in-house executives from across the world) stated that "creativity has taken on a much higher priority over the past 18 months" (PRovoke Media & Now Go Create, 2021).

1.7.1 Areas of specialization

PR can provide solutions to various communication problems, in a specialized way. The following are some of the areas of specialization:

- corporate communications;
- crisis communications;
- internal communications;
- financial and investors relations communications;
- marketing communications;
- media relations;
- content creation;
- events management;
- social media and community management;
- influencer marketing;
- reputation management;
- lobbyism, public affairs and government relations;
- CSR.

However, as we will see in Chapter 4, some of these services are also offered by industries close to PR such as advertising or marketing, and also by professionals such as journalists who go on to work in organizations and specialize in media relations.

The expected areas of growth over the next 5 years, according to ICCO (2021) are strategic consulting, corporate reputation, social media and community management, purpose/CSR, multimedia content creation, and marketing communications.

One of the areas of specialization in PR that has traditionally been associated with creativity is the organization of events. Content creation and storytelling are also perceived as techniques that require large doses of creativity. A study by Estanyol and Roca (2015) identified that the areas of specialization in PR that are most associated with creativity are marketing communication (also called product or consumer communication), the organization of events and digital communication. Areas, on the other hand, where there is greater competition from advertising agencies. However, as reiterated by Palea (2010), all PR techniques can benefit from applying creative ideas.

Let us not forget that, in addition, the PR industry offers its services to companies from different sectors, and this leads to the existence of specializations such as financial communication, pharmaceutical communication, etc. In this regard, according to the study conducted by ICCO (2021), some of the economic sectors that allowed for greater growth in PR in 2021 were

Technology, Healthcare, Financial and Professional Services, Consumer Products, Food and Beverage, and the Public Sector.

1.7.2 A female-dominated industry but not yet led by women

The PR industry is dominated by women, who make up 67% of its total workers. However, as pointed out by the association Women in PR (n.d.), management positions are still held mostly by men, with only 30% of women managers in PR.

The studies that have been carried out for years on women in PR indicate that some of the main issues are salary differences, the glass ceiling, and stereotyped expectations about leadership style, which are generally associated with masculine traits (Tench et al., 2017; EUPRERA, n.d.).

Given this panorama, equity and promoting diversity are cornerstones of the present and the future of the profession.

1.7.3 The structure of the PR sector

PR activity is concentrated in the communication departments integrated within companies and institutions (in house), in the specialized communication and PR agencies and consultancies, and in freelance that provide services in an outsourced manner. They are described in more detail in the following.

1.7.3.1 Integrated communication departments

If we look at the in-house (or integrated) communication departments within organizations, we should specify that they can vary greatly in terms of their structure, size, and position with respect to other departments. The head person in charge of communication is usually the director of communication. Although in the past the director of communication would report to the director of marketing, it is becoming increasingly more common for him/her to be part of the of the dominant coalition (the group of professionals with managerial roles within the organization and who participate in decision making), that is, they report directly to the CEO of the organization. This is evidenced by the results of the report, The Evolving Communication Function, prepared by the Institute For Public Relations (IPR, 2021a) with the participation of 318 PR professionals, among which 33% stated that they reported directly to the CEO, Executive Director, or president of the organization, 22% indicated that they reported to the Chief Communications Officer (CCO) or another communication leader, and 17% indicated that they reported to the Chief Marketing Officer (CMO) or another marketing leader.

The communication departments integrated in organizations can consist of one single person or be made up of a team of more than 50 professionals. One peculiarity is that its size is not always linked to the size of the company, but rather to the importance it places on communication. The size and characteristics of the communication department will depend on various factors: the type of organization (whether it is a private company, public administration, or a nonprofit entity); what the business objectives are, etc.

Within a communication department we can find different areas, for example: the internal communication department, the digital communication department, the press office, etc. In some communication departments, the figure of the creative director already exists, although, as we will see in Chapter 2, this is not yet widespread.

According to data from the study by the IPR (2021a), the main functions carried out by PR professionals are media relations (86%), social media (80%), and crisis/risk communication (75%). Other often-mentioned responsibilities included employee communication (69%), brand building (69%), executive communication (64%), and community relations (58%). The study also points out that the communication function is most frequently combined with marketing, and, although to a lesser extent, with human resources as well.

1.7.3.2 Public relations consultancies

Aside from the communication departments integrated in organizations, PR activity is also performed in communication and PR consultancies These companies can refer to themselves with different names: PR firms, communication consultancies, strategic communication agencies, etc. At the theoretical level, some authors prefer using the term consultancy, instead of agency, alleging that with this name, it better distinguishes them from the press agent model and from advertising agencies (Jefkins, 1993; Wilcox et al., 2012).

These companies can act as a reinforcement of the communication department that already exists in an organization or, in the event that the organization does not have this department, they can take charge of all the planning and execution of PR programs. A PR firm is independent from the client and provides a third-party perspective on the client's business, goods, and services.

PR consultancies can be national or multinational companies, operate locally or internationally, specialize in one area of PR, or offer full services, and have a few employees or hundreds. The origin of the PR multinationals is found in the 1970s in the United States, where they started to expand first to the Anglo-Saxon countries and then to the rest of the world.

Within the PR consultancies we usually find account assistants, account executives, and account directors, who are responsible for planning and executing communication actions for their clients. It is important to note that the figure of the creative director has been incorporated into PR consultancies in recent years; going from being present in 12% of them in 2013, to 53% in 2021 (The Holmes Report & Now Go Create, 2013; PRovoke Media & Now Go Create, 2021).

There are rankings that are published periodically on the sector of PR agencies at an international level with the highest level of turnover, including those prepared by the magazines *PR Week*, *PRovoke*, and *O'Dowyer PR*. Some of the international agencies that usually appear in these rankings are Edelman, Weber Shandwick, BCW, FleishmanHillard, Ketchum, Brunswick, MSL, BlueFocus, Real Chemistry, H+K Strategies, Ogilvy PR, Golin, ICF Next, FTI Consulting, Havas PR Global Collective, Finsbury Glover Hering, MC Group, Vector Inc., Teneo Holdings, WE Communications, APCO Worldwide, Sunny Side Up Inc, Syneos Health, Finn Partners, ICR, Porter Novelli, GCI Health, FischerAppelt, SEC Newgate, etc., among others.

Globalization in the PR industry has meant that in recent years a large number of national consultancies have been acquired by multinationals Bourne (2016). In fact, many of the aforementioned PR consultancies are, at the same time, part of holding companies or large communication groups that also integrate advertising agencies and media centers, some of the largest being Omnicom Group, Publicis, WPP, Interpublic Group of Companies, Dentsu Group, and Havas Group.

However, up against the full-services agencies, there are also independent consultancies, some under the name of creative boutiques. These are smaller agencies, which do not usually have a presence around the world, are highly specialized, and have teams selected for their creative talent. These agencies offer more customized services, often across disciplines, so they develop communication campaigns that can include PR, advertising, design, and marketing actions.

Box 1.4   Rankings

Top 10 PR consultancies according to global revenue (2021) as reported by *PRovoke*

(1) Edelman.
(2) Weber Shandwick.

(3) BCW.
(4) FleishmanHillard.
(5) Ketchum.
(6) Brunswick.
(7) MSL.
(8) BlueFocus.
(9) Real Chemistry.
(10) H+K Strategies.

The positions change if we look at the agencies that have won the most awards for creativity. In this case, the top 10 PR agencies according to creative excellence in PR as reported by PRovoke (2021) are

(1) Weber Shandwick.
(2) BCW.
(3) Edelman.
(4) Ketchum.
(5) Golin.
(6) FleishmanHillard.
(7) Ogilvy.
(8) MSL.
(9) LLYC.
(10) H+K Strategies.

1.8 Entrepreneurship in PR

In the current economic ecosystem, self-employment and entrepreneurship are an opportunity within the creative and cultural industries (Kolb, 2020) and, consequently, also for the PR industry and its professionals. Thanks to the advance of new technologies and internet access, the costs to offer PR services are not as high as they were in the past. However, to start a business, having a good idea is not the only thing, but rather, having a good business plan absolutely essential. The starting point is to define the business idea, that is, define the differential value that will be offered. For this, it will be necessary to apply creativity when observing the ecosystem and propose a versatile option that adjusts to the latent demands or needs.

Subsequently, it will be necessary to assess whether this business idea is viable and calculate its profitability. The creation of the business plan will allow for presenting the proposal to possible investors. Apart from seeking private investment and/or loans from financial institutions, it is always interesting to find out if there is public aid to which you can apply, as well as business incubators or start -up incubators in the territory where you want to circumscribe the business. These spaces help start-up companies by offering spaces to work and also by providing financial advice.

The business plan needs to include different sections, among them:

- the business opportunity;
- the mission, vision, and values;
- the value proposition, the differential value with respect to the competition;
- the market analysis of the competition, and of the potential clients;
- the human capital that is available, that is, who is responsible for promoting it (even if it is only the entrepreneur);
- the business, pricing and sales strategy;
- the calculation of the investment necessary to be able to operate and the length of time expected to recover it, as well as a forecast of expenses and income.

This business plan must be written in a clear and concise manner, providing creative ideas, while it must be presented in a visually attractive and persuasive way to key audiences.

1.9 Collaborative creativity

The approach to creativity, as we have seen, was carried out initially and still predominantly, on the characteristics of the creative individual. However, scientists later focused on the individual's environment also, as an influential context when it comes to nurturing or stifling creativity. It is by this approach that the collective nature of creativity pointed out by Jacucci and Wagner (2007) and upon which Willis and Estanyol (2018) reflected on the PR practice, introducing the concept of "second generation" perspective on creativity in PR, "viewing creativity as an intra-personal to an inter-personal ability" (p. 139). From this stance, creativity goes from being a professional quality to an organizational competence, which arises from the interaction between professionals—in this case, from PR—and which requires their leaders to promote interactions and collaborative work.

Promoting diversity and the exchange of knowledge are fundamental when it comes to encouraging collaborative creativity. Paulus et al. (2012) highlight the importance of knowing how to configure teams so that they are capable of solving complex problems and thus foster organizational creativity through a combination of their knowledge, the ability to select the most effective ideas that arise from the group and also be able to implement them. In Chapter 2, we will see how many of the creative techniques are developed in teams.

1.10 The ethical dimension of creativity

As we have seen, creativity and innovation are generally valued as key to the advancement of organizations in terms of competition. However, creativity is also subject to ethical issues, as highlighted by authors such as Baucus et al. (2008); Mumford et al. (2010); and Moran et al. (2014). In fact, although creativity literature scarcely discusses ethics, it's important to debate how to foster and facilitate creativity while guaranteeing an ethical behavior. Some authors, including Wang (2019), have identified a tension between morality and creativity, since morality is conventional and creativity is unconventional, even going as far as identifying more dishonest behaviors among creative personalities. However, we should not confuse morality and ethics.

Ethics refers to the conventional norms that determine the way to behave for the benefit of the social environment, while the norms and customs are regulated more so by morality. Relating moral issues to paid activity implies acting with professional ethics. As reiterated by Gregory and Willis (2013), ethics and morals "are linked and are particularly important for communication leaders who may be called on from time to time to defend an organizational action that conflicts with their own moral code" (p. 73).

As Mai et al. (2015) point out, creative individuals may tend to think outside the box more, which may also mean that they are less concerned about the ethical implications of their ideas. More specifically, Vincent and Kouchaki (2016) argues that it is not only that creative people think outside the box more, but they also tend to think that they deserve a bigger box than everyone else.

PR professionals, and among them also the most creative, must have some ethical principles, in addition to some values in the profession. For this, it is necessary to consult the different ethical and deontological codes prepared by the different professional associations, for example, the Public Relations Society of America (PRSA), The International Association of Business Communicators (IABC) or the International Public Relations Association (IPRA).

Box 1.5

For example, if we take a look at the **IPRA code of ethics** (IPRA, 2020) we will see that it states that PR professionals should act with

- Respect: Applying the principles of the United Nations Charter and the Universal Declaration of Human Rights, such as equality and the need for inclusion and respect for diversity.

- Honesty and integrity: So as to secure and retain the confidence of those with whom the practitioner comes into contact.
- Dialogue: To recognize the rights of all parties involved to state their case and express their views.
- Transparency: Explaining the interests they represent.
- Avoid any professional conflicts of interest, disclosing such conflicts to affected parties when they occur.
- Confidentiality.
- Truth and accuracy: Not intentionally disseminate false or misleading information.
- Avoid deception: Not obtain information by deceptive or dishonest means.
- Disclosure: Not create or use any organization to serve an announced cause, but which actually serves an undisclosed interest.
- Profit: Not sell for profit copies of documents obtained from other organizations.
- Remuneration: Only accepting payment of professional fees from the principal.
- Avoid inducement: Not giving financial incentives, or any other type, to public representatives or the media.
- Avoid improper influence: Not undertake any action which would constitute an improper influence on public representatives or the media.
- Respect toward competitors: Not intentionally injure the professional reputation of another practitioner.
- Professional poaching: Not seek to secure another practitioner's client by deceptive means.
- Employment: Taking care to follow the rules and confidentiality requirements of the organizations one works for.

1.11 Applying creativity in the PR process

Creativity must be applied throughout the entire PR process. A process that has been defined by many authors, one of the first and most accepted being the one proposed by Marston (1963) who, inspired by the classic process of Management by Objectives (MBO) designed by Peter Drucker (1954), named it with the acronym RACE: Research, Action, Communication and Evaluation.

Cutlip et al. (2000) elaborated a similar proposal, describing the PR process as a cyclical problem-solving process, based on four steps:

(1) *research*: Step in which the research is done to determine the characteristics of the communicative problem or opportunity;
(2) *planning*: Step in which, based on the information gathered, the communication program is made, where the target publics, goals, objectives, strategy, techniques, and actions are defined;
(3) *action and communication*: Step in which the actions previously defined in the communication program are implemented;
(4) *evaluation*: Step in which the preparation, implementation and impact of the PR program are evaluated.

The PR planning process should be, from a creative point of view, dynamic and circular, in order to facilitate interconnections and revisions. It is about achieving a state of creative tension to discover connections between previously unrelated elements. To unblock the elements that can limit an analysis without presumptions to the communicative problem or opportunity, the research should be enriched with questions that differ from the conventional ones. As Michalko (2006) highlights, it is necessary to analyze the available information with a new perspective.

To carry out this approach to the communicative problem from a creative approach, it is proposed:

- to analyze the communication situation with an open mind;
- to study the problem from all perspectives;
- to eliminate assumptions. While what has been done in the past in similar situations could have been useful, if the aim is to achieve different results, new approaches will be need;
- temporarily postpone logical judgment and study the problem from an intuitive approach;
- to break the reference framework.

During the research, the organization itself, the starting situation and the key publics are analyzed in communicative terms. It is important to apply social science research methods, whether they are quantitative (surveys, content analysis, etc.), qualitative (in-depth interviews, focus groups, etc.), or mixed methods. A benchmarking will be helpful to analyze the competitors' communication strategies.

A useful tool for defining the starting situation is to conduct a SWOT analysis (Strengths, Weaknesses, Opportunities, and Threats). This is a strategic analysis that, when applied to PR, consists of analyzing the competitive context of the company in terms of its reputation and communication skills, from two perspectives (external and internal):

- *S—strengths*: are an integral part of the organizational communication. These are strengths at the communication level. Things that the organization does particularly well in terms of communication, or in a way that distinguishes it from its competitors. These are the things that must be encouraged.
- *W—weaknesses*: they are also inherent to the organization itself and its communicative profile, elements on which to focus strategies to improve and overcome.
- *O—opportunities*: includes all the aspects that do not depend directly on the organization but that affect it at the communication level. These points are very revealing when it comes to defining relational and communication strategies that allow you to take advantage of them.
- *T—threats*: these are also external elements. Identifying them will help when it comes time to develop communication and relational strategies to counteract them.

In the research phase, stakeholders should also be analyzed, meaning, the groups of people affected by the activities and decisions of an organization and who have a potential impact on its mission and objectives. A useful tool when carrying out this analysis is to create a map of publics.

During the research step, it would be recommended to apply measures to identify and combat creativity blockages (as the ones identified by Simberg, 1971), complete the publics map with a relationships map, apply creativity techniques to analyze the situation in terms of communication and be able to prepare a creative briefing.

The fundamental purpose of research is to reduce uncertainty in decision making. However, it should be not forgotten than insecurity is precisely one of the characteristics of some creative proposals, since they involve breaking with the status quo by proposing unconventional solutions.

Once the research is finished, the planning stage begins, in which the organization's goals and communication purposes are defined—which are more general—in order to later specify the objectives.

As described by Smith (2020), PR objectives can be classified according to their level of progression in terms of the level of persuasion:

- *awareness objectives*, which aim to inform and include exposure to the message, understanding the message, and the retention of the message by the target audience;

- *acceptance objectives*, which aim to create, reinforce, or modify the interest and attitudes of the public toward a brand, a service, or an organization;
- *action objectives*, which seek to create, reinforce, or modify the behavior of the target audience toward an organization or a brand.

When setting goals, it is recommended to follow the SMART characteristics defined by Doran (1981):

- *S—specific*: concrete;
- *M—measurable*: it will be necessary to have the means to be able to measure if the objectives have been met;
- *A—achievable*: it will be necessary for them to be realistic and achievable in the conditions that are available;
- *R—relevant*: that they are aligned with the organization's overall objectives;
- *T—timely*: limited to a certain time.

Once the map of publics is created and the objectives have been set, the key publics, understood as the strategic audiences that are most important for the communication plan, are defined.

One of the most important planning steps in PR is defining the strategy. Gregory (2010) defines the strategy as the principle that will move the planner from where they are now to where they want to be, emphasizing that "is the overall approach that is taken to a program or campaign. It is the coordinating theme or factor, the guiding principle, the big idea, the rationale behind the tactical program" (p. 118). PR strategies can be reactive—especially when we are facing crises—or proactive. In this phase, it is important to add creativity, working as a team and being able to use different creative techniques—like the ones we will see in Chapter 2—to get multiple ideas, from which the ones that best respond to the problem or communicative opportunity will be selected.

Once the strategy is established, the techniques and tactics, understood as the means and methods, are proposed, which are used to implement the strategy (Cutlip et al., 2000). The tactics are more specific than the techniques, they are the "specific initiatives with which the PR professional manages the problems and spontaneous opportunities and avoids obstacles" (Xifra, 2014, p. 159). Examples of techniques are organizing events, relations with the media, sponsorship and patronage, lobbying, public affairs, etc. The way to go about implementing the PR techniques and tactics will also require creativity.

Preparing the messages that are going to be communicated to the different key publics will also be essential. These messages can be rational or emotional. Creativity plays a key role when it comes time to prepare the messages and helps to make them be more informative or persuasive, depending on the desired objective. The objective in this step is to generate attractive and innovative messages that attract the attention and involvement of the publics. The way in which the message is developed and executed is, on many occasions, essential for a successful PR program.

During the planning process, the communication channels that will be used must also be decided. The PESO (Paid, Earned, Shared and Owned) media model, created by Dietrich (2015), can be useful for establishing the PR strategy and choosing one channel or another:

- *P—paid*: the channels in which money is paid to place the message. Message and distribution are controlled by the organization;
- *E—earned*: also known as publicity, is the result of media and social media relations, the published coverage of the by a third party (journalists, bloggers, trade analysts, industry influencers, etc.);
- *S—shared*: the pass-along sharing and commenting upon the message by the community through social channels;
- *O—owned*: the editorial and messages the organization write, publish, and control(for example through their website, newsletters, social media accounts, etc.).

PR planning also includes the proposal of specific actions (scheduled), the preparation of the budget and, finally, the specification of the evaluation methods that will be used to determine if the objectives have been achieved (see Macnamara, 2018).

It is important to point out, in regards to the evaluation stage, that the International Association for the Measurement and Evaluation of Communication (AMEC) has created the Barcelona Principles in 2010, refreshed for 2020 (see AMEC, 2020). These principles establish that:

(1) setting goals is an absolute prerequisite to communications planning, measurement, and evaluation. The founding principle of SMART goals, as a foundation for communications planning has been promoted to an essential prerequisite;
(2) measurement and evaluation should identify outputs, outcomes, and potential impact;
(3) outcomes and impact should be identified for stakeholders, society, and the organization;
(4) communication measurement and evaluation should include both a qualitative and quantitative analysis. This is necessary not just to

quantify, but also to understand how messages are being received, believed, and interpreted;

(5) the EAVs are not the value of the communication. The Equivalent Advertising Value (EAV) do not demonstrate the value of PR work;

(6) holistic communication measurement and evaluation includes all relevant online and offline channels. The AMEC measurement framework promotes clarity across earned, owned, shared, and paid channels to ensure consistency in approach toward a common goal;

(7) communication measurement and evaluation are rooted in integrity and transparency, respecting privacy and correctly managing data collection, to drive learning and insights.

When it comes to evaluating the impact of a PR action, it is important to recognize the difference between measuring outputs, outtakes, and outcomes:

- *Outputs.* This consists of analyzing the number of communication products or services resulting from a communication process. Outputs are a measure of production and distribution. For example, the number of press releases sent to the media, the number of events organized, of tweets written, etc. They are focused more on what the organization does rather than how the program affects the attitude or behavior of the intended audience.

- *Outtakes.* They evaluate the level of awareness, comprehension and retention of the messages that have been disseminated among the target publics. Also, their level of interest, feedback, engagement, etc.

- *Outcomes.* They analyze the impacts that the communication has on the target public. Evaluates the level of trust, changes in attitudes and behaviors of key publics, etc. According to IPR (March 2021b) this is the ultimate goal and related Key Performance Indicators (KPIs) to which leading senior communicators aspire.

The value of creative thinking in PR lies in making it possible to analyze the communication problems of organizations from new, different, original, and effective points of view; and in applying new methods when dealing with the research, planning, execution, and evaluation of PR programs.

References

Almiron, N., & Xifra, J. (Eds.). (2019). *Climate change denial and public relations: Strategic communication and interest groups in climate inaction.* Routledge.

Amabile, T. M. (1983). The social psychology of creativity: A componential conceptualization. *Journal of Personality and Social Psychology, 45*(2), 357–376.

Auger, G. (2021). Rethinking public relations: Persuasion, democracy, and society (3rd edition). *Public Relations Education, 7*(1), 220–226.

Austin, C. (2007). Embracing your firm's right brain: Wake up your inner creativity. *Public Relations Tactics, 14*(8), 16–23. http://search.ebscohost.com/login.aspx? direct=true&AuthType=ip,cookie,url,uid&db=bsh&AN=26163632&lang=es& site=ehost-live

Baucus, M. S., Norton, W. I., Baucus, D. A., & Human, S. E. (2008). Fostering creativity and innovation without encouraging unethical behavior. *Journal of Business Ethics, 81*(1), 97–115.

Boden, M. A. (Ed.). (1996). *Artificial intelligence.* Elsevier.

Bourne, C. D. (2016). Extending PR's critical conversations with advertising and marketing. *Comunicacao, Midia E Consumo, 13*(38), 29–47. http://dx.doi.org/10.18568/cmc.v13i38.1235

Castells, M. (2004). *La era de la información: economía, sociedad y cultura.* Siglo XXI.

Coombs, W. T., & Holladay, S. J. (2007). The negative communication dynamic: Exploring the impact of stakeholder affect on behavioral intentions. *Journal of Communication Management, 11*(4), 300–312.

Csikszentmihalyi, M. (2015). *The systems model of creativity: The collected works of Mihaly Csikszentmihalyi.* Springer.

Cutlip, S. M., Center, A. H., & Broom, G. M. (2000). *Effective public relations.* Prentice-Hall.

Daymon, C. (2001). Cultivating creativity in public relations consultancies: The management and organisation of creative work. *Journal of Communication Management, 5*(1), 17–30.

De Bono, E. (1995). Serious creativity. *Journal for Quality and Participation, 18*(5), 12–18.

Dey, C. (2021, July 24). Habilidades blandas más valoradas en las empresas. *LinkedIn.* www.linkedin.com/pulse/habilidades-blandas-más-valoradas-en-las-empresas-cecilia-dey/?originalSubdomain=es

Dietrich, G. (2015, June 8). How PESO makes sense in influencer marketing (Asia Edition). In *PR Week.* www.prweek.com/article/1350303/peso-makes-sense-influencer-marketing

Doran, G. T. (1981). There's a S.M.A.R.T. way to write management's goals and objectives. *Management Review, 70*(11), 35–36.

Dozier, D. M., & Lauzen, M. M. (2000). Liberating the intellectual domain from the practice: Public relations, activism, and the role of the scholar. *Journal of Public Relations Research, 12*(1), 3–22.

Drucker, P. F. (1954). *The practice of management.* Harper and Row.

Edwards, L. (2018). *Understanding public relations: Theory, culture and society.* SAGE.

Edwards, L., & Hodges, C. E. M. (Eds.). (2016). *Public relations, society and culture. Theoretical and empirical explorations.* Routledge.

Elmer, P. (2007). Unmanaging public relations: Reclaiming complex practice in pursuit of global consent. *Public Relations Review, 33*(4), 360–367. https://doi.org/10.1016/j.pubrev.2007.08.015

Estanyol, E., & Roca, D. (2015). Creativity in PR consultancies: Perception and management. *Public Relations Review, 41*(5), 589–597. https://doi.org/10.1016/j.pubrev.2014.08.004

European Public Relations Education and Research Association (EUPRERA). (n.d.). *Women in public relations.* https://euprera.org/what-we-do/projects/women-in-public-relations/

Ferrari, M. A. (2013). Las Relaciones Públicas como función de management. *Conference Universidad de La Matanza Buenos Aires.* www.researchgate.net/publication/273886757_Las_Relaciones_Public as_como_funcion_de_management

Fitch, K. (2016). Feminism and public relations. In J. L'Etang, D. McKie, N. Snow, & J. Xifra (Eds.), *The Routledge handbook of critical public relations* (pp. 182–199). Routledge.

Fitch, K., James, M., & Motion, J. (2016). Talking back: Reflecting on feminism, public relations, and research. *Public Relations Review, 42*(2), 279–287.

Gardner, H. (2004). *Frames of mind: The theory of multiple intelligences.* Basic Books.

Golen, S. (1983). How to teach students to improve their creativity in a basic business communication class. *Journal of Business Communication, 20*(3), 46–57.

Green, A. (2009). *Creativity in public relations.* Kogan Page Publishers.

Gregory, A. (2008). Competencies of senior communication practitioners in the UK: An initial study. *Public Relations Review, 34*(3), 215–223.

Gregory, A. (2010). *Planning and managing public relations campaigns: A strategic approach.* Kogan Page Publishers.

Gregory, A., & Willis, P. (2013). *Strategic public relations leadership.* Routledge.

Grunig, J. E. (1992). *Excellence in public relations and communication management.* Lawrence Erlbaum.

Grunig, J. E., & Hunt, T. (1984). *Managing public relations.* Hartcourt Jovanovich College Publishers.

Guilford, J. P. (1950). Creativity research: Past, present, and future. *American Psychologist, 5*(1), 444–454.

Hallahan, K. (1999). Seven models of framing: Implications for public relations. *Journal of Public Relations Research, 11*(3), 205–242.

Heath, R. L. (2006). Onward into more fog: Thoughts on public relations' research directions. *Journal of Public Relations Research, 18*(2), 93–114.

Heath, R. L. (2018). Fully functioning society. In R. L. Heath & W. Johansen (Eds.), *The international encyclopedia of strategic communication.* John Wiley & Sons, Inc. https://doi.org/10.1002/9781119010722.iesc0078

Ihlen, Ø. V., & Van Ruler, B. (2009). *Introduction: Applying social theory to public relations.* Routledge.

Institute For Public Relations (IPR). (2021a). *The evolving communication function.* https://instituteforpr.org/wp-content/uploads/The-Structure-and-Perceptions-of-Communication-Functions-Aug-2021.pdf

Institute For Public Relations (IPR). (2021b, March). *The communicator's guide to research, analysis, and evaluation.* https://instituteforpr.org/wp-content/uploads/IPR-Guide-to-Measurement-v12–1.pdf

International Association for the Measurement and Evaluation of Communication (AMEC). (2020). *Barcelona principles 3.0.* https://amecorg.com/es/barcelona-principles-3/

International Communications Consultancy Organization (ICCO). (2021). *ICCO world PR report 2020.* https://iccopr.com/wp-content/uploads/2021/03/ICCO-report-2020-AMENDS-MARCH-2021.pdf

International Public Relations Association (IPRA) (2020). Code of conduct. www.ipra.org/static/media/uploads/code_of_conduct/spanish.pdf

Jacucci, G., & Wagner, I. (2007, June). Performative roles of materiality for collective creativity. In *Proceedings of the 6th ACM SIGCHI conference on creativity & cognition* (pp. 73–82). Association for Computing Machinery, New York, NY, United States.

Jefkins, F. (1993). *Planned press and public relations.* International Textbook Co.

Kent, M. L., & Taylor, M. (2002). Toward a dialogic theory of public relations. *Public Relations Review, 28*(1), 21–37.

Kolb, B. M. (2020). *Entrepreneurship for the creative and cultural industries.* Routledge.

Kotler, P., & Trías De Bes, F. T. (2003). *Lateral marketing: New techniques for finding breakthrough ideas.* John Wiley & Sons.

Leichliter, M. E. (2001). *Creativity: The cinderella of public relations studies* (M.A. Thesis). California University of Pennsylvania.

L'Etang, J. (2009). *Relaciones públicas: conceptos, práctica y crítica.* Editorial UOC.

Macnamara, J. (2018). *Evaluating public communication: New models, standards, and best practice.* Routledge.

Mai, K. M., Ellis, A. P., & Welsh, D. T. (2015). The gray side of creativity: Exploring the role of activation in the link between creative personality and unethical behavior. *Journal of Experimental Social Psychology, 60*, 76–85.

Marston, J. E. (1963). *The nature of public relations.* McGraw-Hill.

McKie, D., & Galloway, C. (2007). Climate change after denial: Global reach, global responsibilities, and public relations. *Public Relations Review, 33*(4), 368–376. https://doi.org/10.1016/j.pubrev.2007.08.009

McKie, D., & Munshi, D. (2007). *Reconfiguring public relations: Ecology, equity and enterprise.* Routledge.

Mednick, S. (1962). The associative basis of the creative process. *Psychological Review, 69*(3), 220–232.

Michalko, M. (2006). *Thinkertoys: A handbook of creative-thinking techniques.* Ten Speed Press.

Miranda, L. (2022, March 7). Vuelan zepelín para visibilizar violencia contra las mujeres en México. *Cultura Colectiva.* https://culturacolectiva.com/estilo-de-vida/8-de-marzo-vuelan-zepelin-para-visibilizar-violencia-a-las-mujeres-en-mexico/

Moran, S., Cropley, D., & Kaufman, J. (Eds.). (2014). *The ethics of creativity.* Springer.

Mumford, M. D., & Gustafson, S. B. (1988). Creativity syndrome: Integration, application, and innovation. *Psychological Bulletin, 103*(1), 27–43.

Mumford, M. D., Waples, E. P., Antes, A. L., Brown, R. P., Connelly, S., Murphy, S. T., & Devenport, L. D. (2010). Creativity and ethics: The relationship of creative and ethical problem-solving. *Creativity Research Journal, 22*(1), 74–89.

Palea, A. (2010). Creativity in public relations. *Professional Communication and Translation Studies, 3*(1–2), 19–24.

Paulus, P. B., Dzindolet, M., & Kohn, N. W. (2012). Collaborative creativity— Group creativity and team innovation. In M.D. Mumford (Ed.), *Handbook of organizational creativity* (pp. 327–357). Academic Press. https://doi.org/10.1016/B978-0-12-374714-3.00014-8

Pieczka, M., & L'Etang, J. (2006). Public relations and the question of professionalism. In J. L'Etang & M. Pieczka (Eds.), *Public relations: Critical debates and contemporary practice* (pp. 265 278). Lawrence Erlbaum.

PRovoke. (2021). *Global top 250 PR Agency ranking 2021.* www.provokemedia. com/ranking-and-data/global-pr-agency-rankings/2021-pr-agency-rankings/top-250

PRovoke Media & Now Go Create. (2021). Creativity in PR 2021 global study. *PRovoke.* www.provokemedia.com/ranking-and-data/creativity-in-pr

Public Relations Society of America (PRSA). (2012). *A modern definition of public relations.* www.prsa.org/about/all-about-pr

PwC (2022, January 17). *PwC 20th CEO survey.* www.pwc.com/gx/en/ceo-survey/2017/pwc-ceo-20th-survey-report-2017.pdf

Rhodes, M. (1961). An analysis of creativity. *The Phi Delta Kappan, 42*(7), 305–310.

Saavedra, J. M. (2019). Una nueva ola feminista . . . más allá de# MeToo. Irrupción, legado y desafíos. Políticas Públicas para la Equidad, 2.

Sha, B. L. (2007). Dimensions of public relations: Moving beyond traditional public relations models. In S. C. Duhe (Ed.), New media and public relations (pp. 3–26). Peter Land.

Simberg, A. L. (1971). Obstacles to creative thinking. In G. A. Davis & J. A. Scott (Eds.), Training creative thinking (pp. 123–145). Holt, Rinehart & Winston.

Smith, R. D. (2020). Strategic planning for public relations. Routledge.

Sriramesh, K. (2010). Globalization and public relations. Opportunities for growth and reformulation. In R. L. Heath (Ed.), The SAGE *h*andbook of *p*ublic *r*elations (pp. 691–707). SAGE.

Sriramesh, K., & Verčič, D. (2007). Introduction to this special section: The impact of globalization on public relations. Public Relations Review, 33(4), 355–359.

Sriramesh, K., & Verčič, D. (Eds.). (2019). *The global public relations handbook: Theory, research, and practice* (3rd ed.). Routledge.

Sternberg, R. J. (2006). The nature of creativity. Creativity Research Journal, 18(1), 87–98.

Taylor, M. (2000). Cultural variance as a challenge to global public relations: A case study of the Coca-Cola scare in Europe. *Public Relations Review, 26*(3), 277–293. https://doi.org/10.1016/S0363-8111(00)00048-5

Tench, R., Topić, M., & Moreno, A. (2017). Male and female communication, leadership styles and the position of women in public relations. *Interactions: Studies in Communication & Culture, 8*(2–3), 231–248.

The Holmes Report. (2007). 250 largest global public relations firms, ranked by worldwide revenues. *The Holmes Report, 1*(1), 1–16.

The Holmes Report & NowGoCreate. (2013). *Creativity in PR. A global study.* https://es.slideshare.net/ArunSudhaman/creativity-in-pr2013

Toth, E. L. (2010). Reflections on the field. In R. L. Heath (Ed.), The SAGE handbook of public relations (pp. 711–722). SAGE.

Vincent, L. C., & Kouchaki, M. (2016). Creative, rare, entitled, and dishonest: How commonality of creativity in one's group decreases an individual's entitlement and dishonesty. *Academy of Management Journal, 59*(4), 1451–1473.

Wakefield, R. I. (2010). Why culture is still essential in discussions about global public relation. In R. L. Heath (Ed.), The SAGE handbook of public relations (pp. 659–670). SAGE.

Wang, L. (2019). Creativity as a pragmatic moral tool. *Journal of Business Research, 96*, 1–13.

Wilcox, D. L., Cameron, G. T., & Xifra, J. (2012). *Relaciones públicas: estrategias y tácticas.* Pearson.

Willis, P., & Estanyol, E. (2018). Collaborative creativity, leadership and public relations: Identifying and addressing research limitations. In *Public Relations and the Power of Creativity.* Emerald Publishing Limited.

Women in PR. (n.d.). *What we do.* https://womeninpr.org.uk/what-we-do/

Xifra, J. (2014). *Manual de Relaciones Públicas e Institucionales.* Tecnos.

Xiong, Y., Cho, M., & Boatwright, B. (2019). Hashtag activism and message frames among social movement organizations: Semantic network analysis and thematic analysis of Twitter during the# MeToo movement. *Public Relations Review, 45*(1), 10–23. https://doi.org/10.1016/j.pubrev.2018.10.014

Yang, A., & Taylor, M. (2013). The relationship between the professionalization of public relations, societal social capital and democracy: Evidence from a cross-national study. *Public Relations Review, 39*(4), 257–270. https://doi.org/10.1016/j.pubrev.2013.08.002

2 Creativity in public relations

2.1 The importance of creativity in the PR industry

Against today's backdrop of never-ending change, the PR industry is becoming keenly aware of how important creativity is in developing effective campaigns that get key messages across to their target audiences. Yet, as noted by Parker, Wayne, and Kent Ltd. (2005), "creativity is a buzzword that is thrown around the PR industry freely, with little consideration for what it really means and how one might achieve it" (p. 2). The industry seems to agree that creativity is a positive asset. Rawel (2002), for example, suggested that it can add value to PR programs, while Parker, Wayne, and Kent Ltd. (2005) described it as "that 'X factor' which can make a PR programme sparkle" (p. 2). However, there is still a great deal of uncertainty about how to boost and incentivize this important quality in PR.

For Green (2010), creativity in PR means unpacking new ideas that shake up the industry's tried-and-trusted theories, formulas, and routines. The author encourages PR professionals to choose from outside the box of normal and obvious proposals. Also in reference to PR, Sitzman (1980) claimed that "creativity is the capability of producing original work or solving problems on the job" (p. 16). Years earlier, Lesly (1966) had already pointed out that

> real creativity in public relations involves deep analysis of the world the client lives in and must develop in-systematic planning to gear the client's interests into the trends of the public's interests and long-range, permanent actions and communications to bring the attitude of the two together (p. 16)

concluding that the best PR actions are those that fulfill two conditions: (1) they communicate the characteristics of the client's product or service to the target audience, highlighting the points of interest for the latter; and (2)

DOI: 10.4324/9781003246879-2

they benefit the client in a real and practical way, such that their investment in PR pays off.

Fortunately, the PR industry has been publishing more and more studies on the topic, and research endeavors in the field of PR have also begun to spring up in the world of academia, putting creativity under the lens of scientific study. To give an example, *PRovoke* (formerly *The Holmes Report*) has been conducting with Now Go Create an international study called "Creativity in PR" since 2012. By surveying senior professionals in PR firms, consultancies and corporate communication departments across the globe, it is able to shed light on creativity's place in PR. According to the report's most recent issues, the PR industry is becoming increasingly aware of creativity's key role in communication campaigns and actions, but risk aversion among clients continues to put a damper on its potential. The report also reveals that techniques for generating and assessing creative ideas are not fully implemented across the industry and that some of the creative talent of PR professionals has yet to be developed.

2.2 Creativity and strategy

In PR, creativity and strategy must go hand in hand. It is the only way to come up with truly effective solutions that cover organizations' communication needs. These two aspects are often mistakenly set against each other, when in fact they should form a united front in the design of PR projects. Without thoroughly analyzing the baseline situation, setting clear communication goals or determining how these are going to be assessed, an idea will not be effective, no matter how new and original it may be. The takeaway? Creativity without strategy is pointless. What PR needs is creative strategy, a set of communication techniques for crafting messages and carrying out actions that spark interest among stakeholders and sway their opinion in the organization's favor. In this way, creative strategies not only consider the intended message, but also the best way to adapt and deliver that message to the organization's target audiences.

2.3 Creative ideas and their assessment

Creativity in PR can be assessed by looking at the outcome (the PR proposal, program, or action) or by measuring the creative abilities of the professionals involved.

This assessment must be done at every stage of the process: (1) in the initial proposal stage before the team presents its ideas to the promotor (or client), when subjectivity and intuition can pose a problem; (2) in the preimplementation stage, when a focus group with stakeholders can be set up, for example; and (3) in the final stage, when the PR program is implemented. In order to measure audience impact, it is advisable to apply both quantitative and qualitative research methods, as seen in Chapter 1.

Moriarty (1997) used four adjectives to describe creative ideas in PR: risky, relevant, impactful, and original. (1) Risky, because PR professionals must be able to step away from traditional strategies and venture into unknown, untried territory; (2) relevant, because the outcome must be something meaningful for the target audience; (3) impactful, because the idea must be anything but ordinary, obvious, or predictable; and (4) original, because it must be new, fresh, and unexpected. Meanwhile, according to El-Murad and West (2004), creative ideas must be original, imaginative, goal-directed, and problem-solving.

With regard to their creative outcome, scientists agree that ideas must be more than just new and original to be creative. They must also be effective and context-appropriate, which in PR means solving an organization's communication problem or capitalizing on a communication opportunity.

McKinnon (1962), for example, claimed that true creativity is a process that fulfills at least three conditions: (1) it involves a new or statistically rare idea or response; (2) the idea conforms to reality, solving a problem, or achieving a goal; and (3) this original idea is tested and developed until it is implemented. Csikszentmihalyi (1999) pointed out that proponents of creative ideas must be able to convince experts in the field (or domain) of the significance and value of the ideas' novelty.

Assessing creativity in PR can be accomplished by using a rubric that takes into consideration its various dimensions: originality, visibility, effectiveness, engagement, implementation, appropriateness, and stakeholder impact (see Table 2.1).

There are a number of tests available for measuring an individual's creative potential, most of which have been developed within the field of psychology. Case in point are the divergent thinking tests developed by Guilford (1967) and his partners Merrifield, Gershon, and, later, Torrance, which identify verbal and associative fluency.

Another popular creativity test is the Remote Associates Test put forth by Mednick (1962). In it, the person being tested is shown three seemingly unrelated words and is asked to think of a fourth word that is somehow related to each of the first three. This test measures the person's ability to associate ideas, one of the widely recognized traits of creative thinkers.

Ellis Paul Torrance (1968), building on the creativity dimensions proposed earlier by Guilford (1967), created the Torrance Tests of Creative Thinking to assess an individual's creativity on four scales: originality, fluency, flexibility, and elaboration. As Davis and Scott (1984) noted, the creative thinking tests devised by Torrance are possibly the best-known and most carefully researched, and can be used with different age groups and in

Table 2.1 The dimensions of creative ideas and questions to assess them

Dimensions	Questions	Poor	Fair	Good	Excellent
Originality	Is it new and innovative in PR? Is it different, surprising, unique?				
Visibility	Is it impactful? Will stakeholders remember it?				
Effectiveness	Is it right for the intended communication goals? Is it relevant?				
Engagement	Does it create a meaningful link with stakeholders?				
Implementation	Is it developed enough? Does its implementation have quality features?				
Appropriateness	Is it a good way to handle the communication problem/ opportunity at hand? Is it aligned with the organization's mission, vision, and values? Will its implementation stay within budget?				
Impact	Is it able to reinforce or change stakeholders' knowledge, attitude or behavior? Does it have a positive impact on the organization's reputation?				

Source: Author's own work

many different settings. Therefore, it would stand to reason that they could also be used to test the creativity of PR professionals.

2.4 The creative professional

Creativity research has focused a lot of its effort on answering one question: What traits do creative people have that make them that way? These scientific contributions agree that people cannot be classified as creative or noncreative, but that creativity is in everyone to some degree. De Bono (1995) noted that one of the reasons why more academic attention has not been devoted to creativity is this misconception among part of the population that creativity is an almost mystical quality that only some people possess. On the contrary, according to this and many other authors, creativity is not a gift at all, but rather a skill that can be practiced, cultivated, and ultimately improved by anyone, which of course includes PR professionals.

Regarding the factors behind a person's level of creativity, some authors suggest that it depends on IQ, some argue that it is conditioned by certain personality traits, and some believe it is a by-product of both. Now, a growing number of experts are turning to the idea that a person's creative development is strongly influenced by the educational, social, and economic context in which they grow up. The studies by Amabile (1983), Csikszentmihalyi (1999), and Sternberg and Lubart (1997) all focus on how a person's environment can either boost or hamper creativity.

Gardner (1995) posited that creative individuals are those who regularly solve problems, devise products, or define new questions in a field in a way that is considered novel at first but that ultimately becomes accepted in a particular cultural setting. The author claimed that creative individuals are not usually so across the board, but rather uniquely excel in one specific area. In this regard, Gardner's famous theory of multiple intelligences proposes seven different types: visual-spatial, musical, bodily-kinesthetic, logical-mathematical, linguistic-verbal, intrapersonal, and interpersonal.

One of the first scholars to study the creative personality was Taylor (1959), who proposed the following defining traits: curiosity, the desire to manipulate objects, the ability to perceive problems, and the ability to structure preestablished ideas differently. Likewise, McKinnon (1962) and Fiedler and Barron (1967) associated creativity with intuition, sensitivity, and cognitive flexibility.

After a series of studies, Guilford (1967) drew up a list of skills that creative people possess. As seen earlier, Torrance (1968) later proposed how to assess them. They were:

- *Fluency*: the ability to produce many ideas, concepts, or answers when faced with a question or problem;
- *Flexibility*: the ability to handle and produce different types of information and ideas, and the ability to look at things from other angles;
- *Originality*: the ability to come up with new ideas that differ from others;
- *Elaboration*: the ability to think through and carry out concepts or ideas;
- *Sensitivity*: the perceptive quality to recognize problems at their origin, as well as receptiveness to changes in one's surroundings;
- *Redefinition*: the ability to restructure perceptions and concepts, in order to understand or use ideas or objects differently than before.

Csikszentmihalyi (1999) found some common traits among creative people: having clear goals, balancing challenge and skill, displaying intense concentration when in action, refraining from off-course thoughts, and not being afraid of failure. Vervalin (1992) also observed traits shared by individuals of the creative type: a high IQ, an openness to experience, an absence of inhibition and stereotyped thoughts, esthetic sensitivity, and flexibility. According to the author, such individuals also find pleasure in the creative process and are relentless in their search for new challenges and solutions. Sternberg (2006) highlighted other creative personality traits: a willingness to overcome obstacles, the ability to take risks, the ability to tolerate ambiguity, and self-confidence. For this author, being creative also means being able to work on a project or task for a long time without immediate reward. With regard to the PR industry, Moriarty (1997) pointed out that creative professionals must also be disciplined and work well under pressure, as they have to deal with deadlines and client demands. Finally, Sitzman (1980), defined creative PR professionals as assertive, curious, independent, enthusiastic, and courageous enough to face new challenges and take risks without fear of criticism or failure.

2.5 Motivation and flow

For Sternberg (2006), creativity is as much a decision about and an attitude toward life as it is a matter of ability. The author conceptualizes creativity as a choice, saying that not everyone is willing to risk challenging the status quo in their professional field or area of knowledge. Under his view, moreover, people who are brilliantly creative in an activity (whether vocational or not) are almost always truly passionate about what they do.

This is why motivation, especially intrinsic motivation, is such an essential part of creativity. Amabile (1998) described this motivation as allowing people to engage in an activity for their own pleasure because it is intrinsically interesting, enjoyable, or satisfying. With this type of motivation, creation is both the means and the end in itself. Then there is extrinsic motivation, which is shaped by one's environment and serves to reach some external goal, such as recognition or financial reward (Romo, 2009). Creativity is enhanced when extrinsic motivation and intrinsic motivation meet, as the creative effort is rewarded.

However, motivation alone does not guarantee creativity. According to the theory put forward by Amabile (1998), creativity has three components: experience (technical, procedural, and intellectual knowledge), creative thinking skills (fluency, flexibility, etc.), and motivation (intrinsic and extrinsic).

Therefore, to be creative, a good PR professional must have:

- *Experience* (possessing essential knowledge and knowing how to carry out the communication process, as seen in Chapter 1);

- *Creative thinking skills* (fluency, flexibility, originality, elaboration, sensitivity, and redefinition); and
- *Motivation*, both intrinsic (because they like their work) and extrinsic (because they work in an environment where they feel comfortable, recognized, and/or satisfied with their position, pay, etc.).

Csikszentmihalyi (1990) contributed another important concept for understanding and enhancing the creative process: flow. The author described flow as a state in which creators are completely absorbed in what they are doing thanks to a profound motivation that dissipates any thoughts unrelated to the task at hand. In a state of flow, creators become so deeply concentrated that they are able to block out their surroundings and any thoughts outside the problem they are trying to solve or the opportunity they hope to explore.

Mindful of this, the PR industry must do its best to enhance workers' motivation (intrinsic and extrinsic) and flow if it wants to boost creativity.

2.6 The creative director

Creative directors are found in organizations and businesses across a wide range of sectors. They work in fashion, in audiovisual production companies, in the video game industry, in music, in design, and in the advertising business. In advertising—the industry closest to PR, as covered in Chapter 4—the rise of the creative director is credited to Bill Bernbach (who worked as an advertising agent from the 1950s to the 1970s), David Ogilvy (who founded Ogilvy & Mather in 1948), and Leo Burnett (who also created his own agency in 1935).

According to Blasco et al. (2010), creative directors must be responsible for results, but also for creating the right climate to achieve them. They must know which heads to put together and which to keep apart. Good creative directors question ideas that have previously been found. They find their edges, help to polish them, and decide to try new approaches or go back to the drawing board.

There is some controversy surrounding the usefulness of creative directors in the PR industry. Some senior executives believe that having one on board is a way to boost creativity in PR consultancies and in-house communication departments. Others argue that creativity is (or should be) a quality possessed by every PR professional, meaning there is no need for this specific creative role.

According to industry data, over the last decade more than half of large PR consultancies have formally embraced the role of creative director. On this, The Holmes Report, Now Go Create and Ogilvy (2017) wrote that the "PR industry is increasingly entrusting creative directors to oversee its ideas and solutions, with a specialist role proving popular as PR firms step up their efforts to lead creative despite lingering client concerns." Following are some of the tasks carried out by creative directors in PR, as found by this study:

- leading teams in developing creative concepts;
- managing talent;
- offering expert creative guidance;
- putting together ideas that solve the organization's communication problems;
- communicating these ideas to higher-ups or clients (if they work at an agency) clearly and convincingly.

2.7 The creative process

The creative process theory that has had the greatest impact on the scientific study of creativity was put forth by English sociologist Graham Wallas (1926) in *The Art of Thought*. Wallas's model has four stages:

- *Preparation*: In this stage, the creative team sets out to study the problem and define all its characteristics. This involves gathering as much information as possible about the phenomenon or problem to be addressed. The preparation stage requires conscious work involving factors such as education and analytical skills.
- *Incubation*: In this stage, the conscious mental work going into solving the problem must be stopped. The aim is to relax the brain so that the subconscious can take over and begin to form associations. The team members can unwind, engage in other activities, listen to music, and so on. This allows their subconscious minds to sort through a myriad of ideas and combinations. Most often these are ruled out, but every once in a while, a promising idea pops up. In the field of neuroscience, Carson (2012) highlighted that taking a break from a problem gives the brain a chance to recover from mental fatigue, forget bad solutions that it might be fixating on, work unconsciously, and focus on parts of the environment that have nothing to do with the problem but can act as clues to finding creative solutions by stimulating connections between fragments of information stored in the brain.
- *Illumination*: This occurs when a promising idea goes from unconscious to conscious. Lubart (2001) noted that this moment is sometimes characterized by an unexpected flash. At the beginning of the 20th century, Austrian philosopher Ludwig Wittgenstein put forward the theory of

the 3 Bs, according to which the bedroom, the bath, and the bus are the three places in which inspiration is most likely to strike, as they offer moments in which the person is neither working nor engaging in a mentally straining activity, so allowing subconscious thoughts to rise up.

• *Verification*: This is a conscious stage in which the idea is assessed, remolded, and developed further.

In the PR process, these phases would not act as isolated moments, but as meta cognitive processes.

Based on the Wallas' model, Green (2010) adds a fifth phase, the *illustration*, which he describes as the moment in which the idea must be defended in front of the person who will decide whether it will be applied or not.

Sternberg (2006), another prominent creativity researcher, created the Propulsion Model, which proposes eight different ways of being creative:

• *replication*: the most basic level of creativity, consisting of replicating a work, idea, or project. It is understood as being different from copying or repeating;

• *redefinition*: rethinking a problem, project, or idea and having the courage to reformulate questions or ideas that are not up to scratch;

• *forward incrementation*: moving an established idea forward, improving on it in the process;

• *redirection*: taking ideas in a new or unexpected direction;

• *reconstruction*: revisiting past ideas and moving forward in a new direction, finding new meanings, interpretations, or applications along the way;

• *reinitiation*: reinventing a field completely;

• *integration*: merging two ways of thinking into one, giving integrative meaning to ideas that were previously seen as incompatible.

2.8 Creative techniques

There are many techniques for boosting creativity. Jaoui (1979) is credited with one of the most scientifically recognized classifications of these techniques:

• *Association techniques*: These techniques are inspired by Mednick's (1962) associationist theory of creativity and use the association of ideas, structures, and dimensions as a creative process. Among these techniques, we find brainstorming, as proposed by Osborn (1953).

• *Analogy techniques*: These are techniques that spark ideas through direct or inverse analogies. They are rooted in psychoanalytical theory and based on the premise that the best solutions come when an individual is in a preconscious state (between unconsciousness and consciousness). Analogy techniques include synectics (Gordon, 1961) and the use of analogies themselves.

- *Combination techniques*: These are techniques that combine association and analogy techniques. Among these techniques, we find morphological-forced connections (Koberg and Bagnall, 1976) and attribute listing (Crawford, 1954).

Another way of classifying creative techniques is by whether they enhance:

- *fluency* (e.g., brainstorming);
- *flexibility* (e.g., analogies);
- *originality* (e.g., forced connections); or
- *elaboration* (e.g., six thinking hats).

The following sections describe some of the creativity boosting techniques that can be used in the PR industry.

2.8.1 Brainstorming

Brainstorming is perhaps the best-known and most widely used technique for stimulating creativity. However, it is rarely applied following the guidelines laid out by its creator, the advertising executive Alex Faickney Osborn, in his 1953 book *Applied Imagination*. He realized that groups of people come up with more and better creative ideas when they follow a few rules. The brainstorming technique was well received by some of the most powerful multinationals of the time. Osborn would go on to set up the International Center for Studies in Creativity, where he taught classes on creative problem solving.

Brainstorming encourages the fluency of ideas most of all, however, it can also be used to enhance flexibility. The purpose of this technique is to come up with as many ideas as possible among a group of between six and 12 people. It is essential that the ideas are not assessed for suitability until after the exercise has finished. As with any creative process, brainstorming is nonlinear. It involves instances of divergence, where multiple ideas are produced, and convergence, where ideas come together and become something more tangible.

Ideas should be allowed to bounce around freely, even if many of them are no good, which is why the moderator is so crucial in this technique. This person should make sure that everyone has a chance to contribute, preventing any one person from offering up too many ideas, which could demotivate the other participants. It is also up to the moderator to ensure that everyone is able to share their ideas without being criticized, that ideas stay in line with the given subject, and that the group does not digress into off-topic chatter. The secretary is also an important figure in brainstorming sessions and should take notes and write down ideas as they come up.

For a brainstorming boost, groups should look for a change of scenery, sit at round tables (which favor interaction), and work with visual items (sticky notes, images, colored markers, etc.). The secretary should write down the ideas on a whiteboard so that everyone can see the progress being made. Brainstorming sessions should ideally last around a half an hour, after which the group can take another 30 minutes to discuss the ideas through reasoned arguments and comparisons and ultimately decide on their suitability. These timings can always be adjusted to fit the problem at hand, however.

Brainstorming is an exciting technique for many people, since every idea has the chance to "win" regardless of its proponent's rank or status. It is not without drawbacks, though. For instance, some people may not choose to jump in, feeling self-conscious about doing so in front of their colleagues and/or superiors.

When the session is over, the participants should be given a few days to add any further ideas that occur to them individually during the incubation period.

2.8.2 Brainwriting

Brainwriting is like brainstorming, except that participants pool their ideas by first writing them down individually. For this technique, a group of between five and eight people is given a certain amount of time to write down ideas. These are then collected by the moderator and discussed and worked on together as a group. The ideas remain anonymous and are discussed without making reference to anyone in particular. As noted by VanGundy (1984), Heslin (2009), and other authors, this technique makes it possible to maintain anonymity, something rather unfeasible in traditional brainstorming sessions where ideas are shared out loud. This gives everyone an equal opportunity to contribute their ideas freely, which takes pressure off the less intrepid members of the group. Likewise, whereas the constant outpouring of ideas in brainstorming sessions can cause participants to lose focus and forget where their ideas were headed, this does not happen in brainwriting, as each individual is left to explore their ideas alone. It is also a plus that all the ideas are perfectly written out, although some of them may be the same.

This technique is also useful when circumstances make it impossible for the group to gather face-to-face (when the participants live far apart, there is no suitable room available, etc.). This has led to the computer-mediated

Table 2.2 Method 635 template

Problem:			
	Idea 1	*Idea 2*	*Idea 3*
Participant 1			
Participant 2			
Participant 3			
Participant 4			
Participant 5			
Participant 6			

Source: Author's own work

collaborative exercise known as electronic brainwriting. According to Michinov (2012), this involves several groups of people proposing ideas on the same topic, usually simultaneously, although it is possible for contributions to be made at different times.

2.8.3 Method 635

Method 635 takes its name from how the technique is carried out. Six participants each write three ideas on a separate piece of paper. After 5 minutes, they each pass their paper to their neighbor, who then has 5 minutes to add three more ideas. This goes on until everyone has written on every piece of paper.

Although similar to brainwriting, this method is unique; in that, it sets a specific number of participants, ideas, and minutes for coming up with them.

Table 2.2 provides a template for this exercise. Each participant writes the problem in the top row. During the first 5 minutes, they write their three ideas in the corresponding columns. As the paper is passed around, the rows are filled with everyone's ideas.

2.8.4 SCAMPER

The SCAMPER technique was suggested by Bob Eberle (1996) as a mnemonic, based on the previous work of Osborn (1953). This technique encourages users to ask themselves seven questions to explore situations from multiple angles. SCAMPER stands for:

- *S—substitute*: This is about changing a place, person, procedure, or idea for another. It answers the question, "What can be replaced?"

- *C—combine*: This is about mixing variables (topics, concepts, ideas, emotions, etc.). It answers the question, "What can be combined?"
- *A—adapt*: This is about adapting something from another context, setting, etc. It answers the question, "Is there anything from elsewhere that can be used for the case at hand?"
- *M—modify*: This is about distorting, changing, or building on something (or a part of that something) and implies a transformation. It answers the question, "What can be modified?"
- *P—put to other uses:* This is about looking for other ways to use a product, process, or service and about discovering hidden possibilities. It answers the question, "Can this be put to other uses?"
- *E—eliminate*: This is about taking away, downsizing, or cutting back on something. It answers the question, "Can anything be eliminated?"
- *R—rearrange/reverse*: This is about rearranging, reversing, undoing, readjusting, and turning things inside out or upside down. It answers the question, "Can anything be rearranged or reversed?"

Here are the steps to follow in a SCAMPER session:

a. Identify the problem or opportunity

This is the natural first step in solving problems or leveraging opportunities in public relations. It is extremely important to pinpoint what is impeding the organization's growth or progress in terms of improving its corporate reputation.

b. Ask the SCAMPER questions

With a solid grasp of the baseline situation, a group of preselected professionals gathers to ask the SCAMPER questions. As with brainstorming, this technique requires a round of judgement-free idea sharing. Critiquing should be saved for a later stage in the creative process, where ideas are sorted by suitability. The flow of ideas can become stifled otherwise.

c. Organize the ideas

All the resulting ideas should be compiled, without censoring or criticizing any of them.

d. Assess the ideas

This is the time to single out the top ideas and rule out others. The group should come to an agreement about which ideas are best suited to solve the problem or seize the opportunity at hand, and which missed the mark.

f. Formally select the best ideas

In this last step, the ideas that best fit the target problem or opportunity are formally selected. The group should write up a justification of their decision, laying out the reasons why said ideas should be applied.

Box 2.1

The **"Raising awareness of endangered species"** campaign launched by Lacoste offers an applied example of the SCAMPER technique, specifically the S (substitute) step. Teaming up with the International Union for Conservation of Nature (IUCN) and BETC Paris (Havas Group), the company created "Save our species", a limited collection of polo shirts on which the brand's iconic crocodile logo was replaced with 10 endangered species. The number of polo shirts produced with the green-colored images matched the actual number of these animals remaining on the planet. In total, 1,775 polo shirts were distributed in a collection that was presented during Paris Fashion Week. The articles were made available for purchase on the company's website, with the profits going to the protection of these species (Havas, 2018).

Box 2.2

For an example of the C (combine) step, this time dealing with a product, we turn to **Chupa Chups**. The idea came to Catalonia-born Enric Bernat in 1958 when he was looking for a way to keep children's hands from getting sticky when eating candy. It occurred to him to put the candy on a stick, and this sweet treat has existed ever since. Another fun fact is that the logo, still on every wrapper today, was designed by the surrealist artist Salvador Dalí: "The artist is said to have taken only an hour to draw the brand's new logo" (*Cinco Días*, 2015).

Box 2.3

Plenty of cases of A (adapt) came about during the COVID-19 lockdown periods, when many face-to-face events were transformed into virtual ones.

For instance, Zara, the Inditex group's multinational clothing company, decided to launch a summer campaign to remind people how important it was to #stayathome. Through the campaign, titled **"Shot from home"**, the brand wanted to prove that many things could be done without leaving the house, including fashion shoots. The brand sent their models the items (cameras, clothing, etc.) they needed to take videos and selfies of themselves inside their homes while donning pieces from the latest collection.

Box 2.4

The **Post-it** is an excellent example of P (put to other uses). The game-changing discovery began in 1968 when Dr. Spencer Silver, a chemist working at 3M, developed a new adhesive. According to Valenzuela (2013), Silver's research was focused on creating strong adhesives for use in the aerospace industry. However, he ended up with a weak product that allowed two sheets of paper to be stuck together and then peeled apart without leaving any residue behind. What was more, the adhesive's microspheres were strong enough to stick to surfaces over and over again. Meanwhile, Arthur Fry, another 3M employee, was frustrated. Once a week, he would use little scraps of paper to mark the hymns that he was going to sing with his Presbyterian church choir in the upcoming service, only to find that they had fallen out of the hymnal by Sunday. It was in one of those moments of frustration in 1971 that he recalled Silver's invention. "I thought, what we have here isn't just a bookmark", said Fry. "It's a whole new way to communicate" (3 M, n.d.).

Box 2.5

To make good use of E (eliminate), PR firms could take a critical look at the events they put on and remove any nonessential items, such as those made of unsustainable materials. The practices of reuse and recycling could be promoted instead (e.g., putting in water fountains rather than giving each attendee a single-use bottle).

Lastly, an example of R (rearrange) might involve switching up one of the communication activities held every year. For instance, instead of inviting everyone on the team to a traditional Christmas dinner, organizing a summer get-together someplace special and putting on activities that impress everyone there.

2.8.5 Six thinking hats

First proposed by Edward de Bono (1988), six thinking hats is a technique for investigating an issue (e.g., a PR problem or opportunity) from six different perspectives. Each colored hat represents one of these perspectives. So, as participants "put them on", they adopt a certain role and way of thinking.

- The *white hat* is about giving key information, data, and facts surrounding the issue. The wearer's contributions should be as neutral and objective as possible.
- The *red hat* is associated with feelings, intuition, and emotions. The wearer should avoid explanation, logic, or justification.
- The *black hat* is for analyzing potential risks, weaknesses, problems, dangers, and difficulties. It is logical and cautious. It is about exercising caution and is used for critical judgement.
- The *yellow hat* is about optimism. The wearer looks for benefits, values, and advantages; and focuses on the desired outcomes.
- The *green hat* is associated with possibilities, alternatives, and new ideas and solutions. The wearer is meant to think laterally, coming up with new prospects and hypotheses.
- The *blue hat* is about compiling and organizing all the ideas that come out during the exercise. The wearer oversees the process and delivers summaries, conclusions, and decisions.

The six thinking hats dynamic begins by defining the issue and assigning the blue hat to the person who is going to moderate the session. This person should ideally have leadership skills and the ability to mediate among differing points of view. The remaining five hats are then passed out to the participants, who are asked to contribute to the session according to its color. Participants should not wear any one hat for more than 1 to 3 minutes. This ensures a myriad of opinions in a short amount of time. Before ending the session, the blue hat should wrap up by providing a summary of the contributions.

This technique aids in decision making and provides well-rounded insight into a given issue, thanks to the various approaches, perspectives, and styles of thinking it brings out.

Box 2.6

In 2018, more than 600 KFC locations in the United Kingdom ran out of chicken, prompting a necessary crisis communication response.

The restaurant chain had to figure out how to apologize to its customers. According to Mother London (2018), the firm responsible for the response, the angle was to be honest, add a dose of humor, and send out a sincere apology. To do so, they swapped the chain's initials (KFC) around to say "FCK", followed by **"We're sorry."**

The message and image soon went viral on social media, garnering empathy from regular customers while also creating a much wider audience impact.

2.8.6 Mind mapping

Mind mapping is another highly well-known technique for stimulating creativity. Mind maps were first described by Buzan in 1974 (more detailed in Buzan, 2006). They are the result of drawing synoptic tables and diagrams of ideas related to a central topic. Mind mapping encourages the brain to abandon linear thinking, allowing connections to be made that may not otherwise be apparent.

The center of the map is for the idea or image that symbolizes the creative focus or the central concept to be worked on; it is called the central node. Secondary ideas branch out from there. Other essential elements on mind maps are idea connectors, colors, and depictions of concepts as images or drawings.

Mind maps allow users to see a lot of information at a glance. They can be made on paper, on a whiteboard, or using specially created online tools.

2.8.7 PO: provocative operation

Provocative operation (PO) is another technique that was proposed by De Bono. The purpose of provocation is to stray from the usual path of thought, to step away from deductive and structured ways of thinking, and to stimulate lateral thinking instead. Provocation is a kind of thought experiment. It is about deliberately producing an idea that pushes the boundaries of what is reasonable for our experience, becoming an alternative to a hypothesis. According to De Bono (1995), provocation introduces instability and allows us to achieve new stability.

This technique involves coming up with provocations, or nonsensical statements, that encourage people to think outside the box. The point of provocation is to divert the mind from its usual path of thought. Users start by analyzing something (a topic, an item) as if it were the first time. The provocation comes by uttering a sentence that seems completely impossible.

An example given by De Bono himself is "cars have square wheels." The provocation shocks people into thinking outside the usual limits of logic and reason. Although the provocation itself is not considered a valid idea, it provides an original starting point for creative thinking. The aim is to gradually work the provocation into a different, useable idea. It is about moving forward from the provocation until you land on something new. Provocations are not to be justified. Going back to the example, De Bono argues that if cars had square wheels, they would not be able to move because the bumps in the ground would make it impossible for them, but this can trigger thoughts about the importance of suspension systems and ways to improve them.

Box 2.7

A **meatless burger** could be an example of provocative operation. Burger King launched the "Impossible Whopper" in the United States, one of the world's biggest consumers of meat. The communication campaign kicked off in St. Louis on April Fools' Day, with a social media strategy using the tagline, "100% Whopper, 0% Beef." Many consumers who tried the burger for the first time shared their experience on social media, which generated significant visibility both in the U.S. and abroad.

Box 2.8

The **Walk of Shame on EU–Parliament** is another possible example of provocative operation. On August 15, 2015, activists rolled out a 100-meter-long list that included the names of 17,306 human beings who drowned in the Mediterranean between 1990 and 2012 while attempting to migrate. The list was laid out on the EU–Parliament floor like a carpet so that the MEPs had to walk over it. The act raised visibility and awareness around this humanitarian problem.

2.8.8 Synectics

The word "synectics" comes from Greek and means "the joining together of different and apparently irrelevant elements." The synectics technique was developed by William Gordon (1961), based on the conviction that creation and invention are unconscious and irrational in origin. This ties back to the creative process's incubation and illumination stages seen earlier in this chapter. The technique seeks to use unconscious mechanisms grounded in logic and reason to look for solutions in all possible directions. It involves the spontaneous association of words, images, and ideas and draws on the relationship between the rational and the irrational.

This technique also uses analogies. Instead of attacking a problem head-on, it is compared to other things to find possible solutions. It is about looking for similar attributes in different objects or beings. The point is to identify solutions that have been used to solve similar problems in other contexts.

There are four basic operational mechanisms in synectics:

- *Direct analogy* focuses on making connections between the problem and an object or circumstance. One could ask, "What would I find in an environment that resembles this problem?" It is about looking to nature for possible solutions. In fact, many products have been invented this way, such as swimming suits that mimic sharkskin and wingsuits, which have a flying squirrel-like design.
- *Symbolic analogy* uses metaphors and symbolic images. It involves asking the question, "If the problem were a. . . , what would it be like?" The point is to come up with condensed, poetic statements based on the problem or situation being addressed.
- *Personal analogy* is about identifying with the problem on a personal level. It helps to ask, "What human traits could this item have?" or "How would the problem feel if it were human?"
- *Opposite analogy* involves looking for pairs of opposites that describe the situation.
- *Fantasy analogy* swaps the problem out for a fantasy, something outside the confines of reality. Freedom is given to openly express outlandish thoughts that go against all common sense. It involves asking the question, "How would we like this to work?"

As noted by Lanigan (1999), synectics employs the strategy of making the familiar strange and the strange familiar.

This technique can be carried out individually or in groups of between five and seven people. The participants must be ready to tolerate ambiguity; this, as we have seen earlier, is one of the skills shown by creative people. The aim is to incentivize the ability to cope with complexity and (apparent) contradiction, as well as to foster a state of free thinking where analogies between perceptions, concepts, and fantasies are created.

Box 2.9

An analogy of conquest. "Iwo Jima McDonald's" is a piece by street artist Fukt from 2011, located in Sydney, Australia. It is a parody of the iconic WWII photo "Raising the Flag on Iwo Jima" (Joe Rosenthal, 1945) as it substitutes the U.S. flag with a McDonald's sign. "In protest of this overwhelming "McDonaldization" of society, a term first coined in 1993 by sociologist George Ritzer, artists around the world have created some highly vivid pieces that assail the symbols of McDonald's omnipresence". . . . This piece depicts "American's military hegemony and its cultural dominance, suggesting that U.S. power is exerted abroad for the benefit of the country's corporations" (Short, 2014).

2.8.9 Attribute listing

Developed by Robert P. Crawford in 1954, attribute listing is a technique for stimulating creativity and generating ideas. The point is to come up with creative ways to improve a product, service, or process. The first step is to draw up a list of attributes. These can refer to something's physical traits (size, dimension, etc.), its functions, its look and feel (color, shape, etc.), and its usefulness. Other qualities such as its applications, synonyms, antonyms, components, and connotations should also be considered, so as to come up with the maximum number of attributes possible. The next step is to analyze each attribute individually and ask questions about how to improve it. This turns every item on the list into a jumping-off point for change and betterment with regard to the given situation, object, or process.

When designing a recurring PR action, we can make a list of attributes by analyzing each of its components and looking for ideas to improve it. This could be:

- the communication channel used;
- the type of message; or
- the target audience.

This can spark ideas for tweaking one or more of these components, which as a result will change the action for the better.

Box 2.10

The Plastic Oceans Foundation, LADBible and AMVBBDO launched a communication campaign called **"The Trash Isles"** in 2018 to lobby the UN to officially recognize the France-sized mound of trash floating in the Pacific Ocean as a new country. The initiative sought to raise awareness among governments and citizens around the world about the pressing need to curb ocean pollution and ensure that this country of trash is the first and last to ever exist. LAD Bible Group (n.d.) said: "We created The Trash Isles identity including an official flag, currency called "Debris", and passports created from recycled materials."

They also created videos and shared them on YouTube. Well-known figures such as David Attenborough, Chris Hemsworth, Judi Dench, and former U.S. Vice President and environmental advocate Al Gore could be seen showing off their passports. Anyone wishing to join the cause and become a citizen of The Trash Isles could do so on request via Change.org.

2.8.10 Morphological analysis

Morphological analysis is an analytical-combinatorial technique that was developed by Fritz Zwicky in the mid-1940s (see Zwicky, 1948). It involves creating a morphological matrix or grid in which various options are proposed for each aspect of a given item or situation.

This technique is usually carried out in three steps. The first step is to study the problem's morphology or structure, in order to break it down into its most meaningful variables. In step two, the variables are arranged along the axes of a matrix. The final step involves analyzing the boxes, which represent the combination of variables, to look for creative ideas.

Morphological analyses provide numerous combinations, as well as other permutations that have not yet been explored. This kindles the imagination and yields a wealth of data.

As Michalko (2006) explained, when the matrix is filled in, random paths are taken along the parameters and variations, selecting one or more from each column and then combining them in entirely new ways. Every combination in the matrix can be examined to see how it affects the subject at hand.

When designing a new product launch, for example, PR firms may need to look for alternative event ideas. They could start by drawing up a list of attributes, which in this case could be duration, venue, target audience, invitation, entertainment, food, etc. They would then need to suggest several options for each of these aspects, arrange them into a matrix (see Table 2.3), and assess all the combinations.

One combination could be "a one-hour event on the beach with a dance performance and Greek food." This idea may not fit the event's objectives, but it can lead to other promising outcomes. Indeed, even if the resulting event idea does not suit the communication needs, it can serve as a

Table 2.3 Example of a morphological matrix

Duration	Venue	Invitation	Entertainment	Food
30 minutes	Hotel	Card	Dance performance	Greek
45 minutes	Park	Email	Musical performance	Italian
60 minutes	Beach	Hand delivery	Magic show	Japanese
90 minutes	Theater	Social media (mass invitation)	Speech	Spanish
120 minutes	Fair	Phone	Fashion show	Mexican

Source: Author's own work

jumping-off point for thinking up other possibilities and putting together a more fitting creative proposal.

2.9 Ten tips for stimulating creativity in PR

Creativity is one of the skills required of PR professionals and is also one of client companies' top criteria when choosing a firm. However, the perception of creativity is still shrouded in certain stereotypes, there is a great deal of controversy surrounding the role of creative directors in PR, the creativity techniques used in the industry are still basically limited to brainstorming, and creativity continues to be associated mainly with consumer-targeted communication.

The academic literature on creativity management, coupled with the results of interviews carried out with creative directors in international PR firms (Estanyol & Roca, 2015), led to the following ten tips for stimulating creativity in the PR industry:

(1) If you are the manager of a PR consultancy or in-house communication department, understand that you must stimulate creativity. This will involve creating a work environment in which people feel free and confident to express their ideas, granting them autonomy to do their work, and properly allocating budgetary resources.

(2) *Take risks*: Creative ideas in PR often breed uncertainty, as they imply designing actions that have never been done before. Managers must foster a climate that tolerates ambiguity and allows time for people to think through new ideas.

(3) *Fight negativity*: Negativity, in its broadest sense, is one of the main stiflers of creativity. Identifying the creativity blockers (avoiding risks, making judgements too quickly, following the same routines, thinking there is just one answer, low confidence, etc.) is the first step in combatting them.

(4) *Bring in a creative director*: The size of communication and PR firms and in-house communication departments often makes it difficult to hire a creative director. In these cases, it is a good idea to designate a current employee as creativity facilitator. Another option is to hire freelance creatives to collaborate with staff.

(5) *Create an atmosphere where creativity can flourish*: This can be accomplished by making organizational changes, switching up work routines, and fostering environments that provide ample flexibility and autonomy. Likewise, it is a good idea to replace traditional team-based setups with new organizational systems where work is done more by role, rather than by sector or PR technique.

(6) *Avoid the risks of hyper-specialization*: Too close a link with the promoter or specialization in one technique or area of PR can make it difficult to achieve the degree of distance necessary to contribute unconventional ideas. It is therefore recommended to rotate teams and apply creativity techniques to encourage creative distance (concept described by Sternberg in 1999).

(7) *Embrace creativity training*: Theorists from the environmental school of creativity suggest that creativity can be stimulated through practice and training. Universities should therefore include this skill in the curriculum of their PR degrees. Likewise, companies in the PR industry should provide creativity training for their in-house teams, for example by organizing creativity workshops, analyzing case studies, or practicing creative techniques.

(8) *Apply creativity techniques other than brainstorming*: Although brainstorming is used as a creative technique throughout the PR industry, it is rarely done correctly. Besides carrying out proper brainstorming sessions, companies should try other techniques that are not so widely used, such as the ones described in this chapter (SCAMPER, six thinking hats, synectics, forced connections, metaphors and analogies, mind mapping, etc.).

(9) *Value diversity*: Having a mix of professionals with varying degrees of expertise and different personality traits is a plus when it comes to finding more creative, out-of-the-box solutions. It is also a good idea to figure out who has what creativity-related abilities (fluency, originality, flexibility, and elaboration) and create teams whose members complement one another.

(10) *Foster extrinsic and intrinsic motivation*: In other words, create a climate that is emotionally stimulating.

In short, creativity must become a part of the organizational culture in PR.

References

3 M (n.d.). *Acerca de la marca Post-it®*. www.3m.com.es/3M/es_ES/post-it-notes/contact-us/about-us/

Amabile, T. M. (1983). The social psychology of creativity: A componential conceptualization. Journal of Personality and Social Psychology, 45(2), 357–376.

Amabile, T. M. (1998). How to kill creativity. Harvard Business Review, 76(5), 77–87.

Blasco, R., Moliné, M., & Sivera, S. (2010). Pensament creatiu: dos hemisferis i una guia. Editorial UOC.

Buzan, T. (1974). Use *your* *head*. BBC Publication.

Buzan, T. (2006). The mind map book. Pearson Education.

Carson, S. H. (2012). Your *creative brain*: Seven *steps to maximize imagination, productivity, and innovation in your life*. Harvard Health Publication. John Wiley & Sons.

Cinco Días. (2015, May 10). *Chupa Chups, el exitoso caramelo con un palito*. https://cincodias.elpais.com/cincodias/2015/05/08/sentidos/1431109210_175620.html

Crawford, R. P. (1954). The techniques of creative thinking: How to use your ideas to achieve success. Hawthorn Books.

Csikszentmihalyi, M. (1990). Flow: The psychology of optimal experience (Vol. 1990). Harper & Row.

Csikszentmihalyi, M. (1999). Implications of a systems perspective for the study of creativity. In R. J. Sternberg (Ed.), Handbook of Creativity (pp. 313–335). Cambridge University Press.

Davis, G. A., & Scott, J. A. (1984). Estrategias para la creatividad. Paidós.

De Bono, E. (1988). Seis sombreros para pensar. Ediciones Granica SA.

De Bono, E. (1995). Serious creativity. Journal for Quality and Participation, 18(5), 12–18.

Eberle, B. (1996). Scamper: Creative games and activities for imagination development. Prufrock Press.

El-Murad, J., & West, D. C. (2004). The definition and measurement of creativity: What do we know? Journal of Advertising Research, 44(2), 188–201.

Estanyol, E., & Roca, D. (2015). Creativity in PR consultancies: Perception and management. Public Relations Review, 41(5), 589–597.

Fiedler, F. E., & Barron, N. M. (1967). *The effect of leadership style and leader behavior on group creativity under stress*. Illinois Univ Urbana Group Effectiveness Research Lab.

Gardner, H. (1995). Multiple Intelligences as a Catalyst. *The English Journal, 84*(8), 16–18.

Gordon, W. (1961). *Synectics*. Harper & Row.

Green, A. (2010). *Creativity in public relations*. Kogan Page.

Guilford, J. P. (1967). *The nature of human intelligence*. McGraw-Hill.

Havas (2018, March 20). *Save our species, Lacoste cede su protagonismo por una buena causa*. https://havasfuturetogether.com/save-our-species-lacoste-cede-su-protagonismo-por-una-buena-causa/

56   *Creativity in public relations*

Heslin, P. A. (2009). Better than brainstorming? Potential contextual boundary conditions to brainwriting for idea generation in organizations. Journal of Occupational and Organizational Psychology, 82(1), 129–145.

Jaoui, H. (1979). Claves para la creatividad. Diana.

Koberg, D., & Bagnall, J. (1976). The *universal traveler*: A *soft systems guide to creativity. problem solving, and the process of design*. W. Kauffman.

LAD Bible Group. (n.d.). *Trash Isles*. www.ladbiblegroup.com/casestudy/trash-isles/

Lanigan, R. L. (1999). Applied creativity in PR and R&D: Peirce on synechsim, fuller on synergetics, Görden on synectics, and Alinksy on socialism. *Semiotics*, 94–106.

Lesly, P. (1966). Real creativity in public relations. *The Public Relations Quarterly, 10*, 8–16.

Lubart, T. I. (2001). Models of the creative process: Past, present and future. Creativity Research Journal, 13(3), 295–308.

McKinnon, D. W. (1962). Personality and the realization of creative potential. American Psychologist, 20, 273–281.

Mednick, S. (1962). The associative basis of the creative process. Psychological Review, 69(3), 220–232.

Michalko, M. (2006). Thinkertoys: A handbook of creative-thinking techniques. Ten Speed Press.

Michinov, N. (2012). Is electronic brainstorming or brainwriting the best way to improve creative performance in groups? An overlooked comparison of two idea-generation techniques. Journal of Applied Social Psychology, 42, 222–243.

Moriarty, S. E. (1997). The big idea: Creativity in public relations. In C. L Caywood (Ed.), The *h*andbook of *s*trategic *p*ublic *r*elations & *i*ntegrated *c*ommunications (pp. 554–563). McGraw Hill.

Mother London. (2018, February 23). *KFC, FCK*. https://motherlondon.com/work/kfc-fck/

Osborn, A. F. (1953). Applied imagination. Charles Scriber's Sons.

Parker, Wayne & Kent Ltd. (2005). *The management of creativity in the public relations process*. www.pwkpr.com/downloads/The_Management_of_Creativity_in_the_PR_Process_PW&K.pdf

Rawel, A. (2002). How far do professional associations influence the direction of public relations education? *Journal of Communication Management, 7*(1), 71–78. https://doi.org/10.1108/13632540310807269

Romo, M. (2009). Psicología de la creatividad. Paidós.

Rosenthal, J. (1945). Raising the flag on Iwo Jima.

Short, K. (2014, April 24). 15 captivating works of art that challenge the McDonaldization of Society. *Huffpost*. www.huffpost.com/entry/mcdonalds-protest-art_n_4981799

Sitzman, M. (1980). Creativity and public relations. *The Public Relations Quarterly, 25*(4), 16–17.

Sternberg, R. J. (2006). The nature of creativity. *Creativity Research Journal, 18*(1), 87–98.

Sternberg, R. J., & Lubart, T. I. (1997). *La creatividad en una cultura conformista: un desafío a las masas*. Paidós.

Taylor, I. A. (1959). The nature of the creative process. Creativity, 51–82.

The Holmes Report, No Go Create & Ogilvy. (2017). *Creativity in PR. A global study*. www.slideshare.net/ArunSudhaman/creativity-in-pr-2017

Torrance, E. P. (1968). *Torrance tests of creative thinking*. Personnel Press.

Valenzuela, A. (2013, September 22). ¿Cómo se inventaron las notas adhesivas? *RTVE*. www.rtve.es/noticias/20130922/como-se-inventaron-notas-adhesivas/749100. shtml

VanGundy, A.B. (1984). Brain writing for new product ideas: an alternative to brain-storming. *Journal of Consumer Marketing, 1*(2), 67–74. https://doi.org/10.1108/eb008097

Vervalin, C. H. (1992). ¿Qué es la creatividad? In G. A. Davis & J. A. Scott (Eds.), Estrategias para la Creatividad (pp. 19–23). Paidós.

Wallas, G. (1926). The art of thought. Jonathan Cape.

Zwicky, F. (1948). *Morphological creativity*. Interscience.

3 Key trends and issues in the PR sector

3.1 Emotion and strategy

In the professional field of PR, there is a growing interest in exploring the factors that influence people's choices and behavior, especially when it comes to organizations' target audiences. Scientific studies have shown that people saturated with information are less likely to react to rational arguments and react instead to messages and stimuli that affect them and spark their imagination. The emotional component of persuasive strategies thus becomes a key aspect to consider when planning communication and PR actions and campaigns. Interest in emotional intelligence applied to PR has also reached the world of academia, where there are studies on the emotional dimension of professional leadership in the sector (Jin, 2010).

If we recognize that PRs' mission is to forge mutually beneficial relationships between organizations and their audiences, it is important to delve deeper into how these relationships are built and how they are influenced by feelings and emotions, two concepts that are often confused. Even so, while emotional communication has been addressed by several authors in marketing and advertising literature (Zeitlin & Westwood,1986; Patti & Moriarty, 1990; Bagozzi et al., 1999), it is quite uncommon to find articles or chapters on this topic in the scientific literature on PR.

Adding to the critical theory of PR, L'Etang (2009) discussed how the discipline's predominantly profession-centered focus stemmed from a logical-rational, functionalist, and technocratic mindset that neglects the emotional nature of communication and views audiences from the perspective of the organization's interests, without giving much thought to the value of relationships themselves.

Thus, when the aim of a PR action or campaign is to cause an emotional response—that is, to get people to like or trust an organization—it is best not to forget the influence of the so-called triune brain. According to this

DOI: 10.4324/9781003246879-3

concept, the brain has three main parts (1) the reptilian complex, the most primitive part responsible for basic survival instincts; (2) the limbic system, the center of emotions and memory storage; and (3) the neocortex, the rational part responsible for conscious thought, emotional control, and cognitive ability. Swaying people's attitude in this way can lead to behavioral changes (conative objective), which are due to a combination of factors: sensory perception, cognitive potential, emotions, sentimental-affective elaborations, imagination, and acquired biological and cultural patterns (Ferreras, 1995).

If we want to better understand the relationship between people's emotions and behavior in PR, we must look to the principles of psychology, the discipline that has studied the matter most extensively. Cognitive psychology posits that emotions influence behavior, while, at the same time, behavior itself triggers emotions (Chóliz, 2005). Thus, although rationality and emotionality are often at odds with one another, scientific studies have shown that when making choices or adopting attitudes, people's rational and emotional thought processes combine (Payne, 1985; Greenspan, 1997; LeDoux, 2000; Mayer et al., 2004). Therefore, even the supposedly rational choices we make are conditioned—albeit often subconsciously—by emotional factors. On this subject, Goleman (1999), who fathered the concept of emotional intelligence, wrote that "a view of human nature that ignores the power of emotions is sadly shortsighted."

Traditionally, emotions have been classified as primary, secondary, and complex, the last of these arising when emotions in the first two categories mix. This creates a broad emotional spectrum that Plutchik (1980) depicted in his wheel of emotions, which uses a color code much like the color wheel itself. During the research phase of the PR process, it is essential to take steps to understand the functions of emotions (adaptive, social, and motivational, according to Reeve, 2010) and to identify the target audience's wants, desires, and aspirations. Only then can a PR initiative achieve its affective objectives, conative objectives, and engagement (a committed relationship between audiences and brands and/or organizations). This lays the groundwork for increasing arousal, that is, the threshold of attention and involvement (Eysenck, 1982).

The emotional side of communication is conveyed through tone, in messages that harness the latest popular techniques such as storytelling, as well as through the actual behavior demonstrated by the organization and its representatives. Thus, beyond one-way mass communication actions, it is the empathy, integrity, honesty, and commitment that organizations show toward certain groups of people or situations that will help boost engagement among their audiences.

Box 3.1

"Choose Your Future" was a campaign launched by the European Parliament to encourage people to vote in the 2019 elections. Its message, "You are in control of your future", sought to boost the public's trust in politics and reduce Euroscepticism. The result: increased voter turnout. The campaign creators wanted to convey a message of hope, which they did by filming the birth of babies in various European countries just before the elections. The campaign received wide media and television coverage in Europe and had a strong social media strategy, personalizing the message and reaching out to all EU Member States (Eurobest, 2019).

Box 3.2

"Show Us". Getty Images, Dove, and Girlgaze created this hashtag so that women around the world could showcase their different body types and support the body positivity movement. The aim was to "change the visual representation of the billions of women portrayed unrealistically in stock photography". Aided by communication consulting firm Golin, the campaign "targeted social influencers as well as traditional media, all localized with relevant talent while a wide-reaching social and digital campaign across Dove owned platforms encouraged women to take part" (Golin, n.d.-b).

3.2　Storytelling

Storytelling is a tool that involves crafting stories or narratives. In PR, it can be used to tell the story of an organization's founders, for instance. The famous biographies of Steve Jobs and Bill Gates as the respective creators of Apple and Microsoft are good examples of this. By telling stories, organizations can forge stronger connections with audiences, hold their attention, and increase their empathy. PR professionals can therefore benefit from strengthening their storytelling skills. Heath (2000), writing from the rhetorical perspective of PR, is among the authors to have highlighted the importance of storytelling to connect with an organization's audiences and gain their trust. Boje (2008) and Elmer (2016) have also pointed out how effective storytelling can be in PR for connecting with audiences on a more intimate level.

Storytelling can be used for both external and internal communication. For Gill (2011), the qualities of storytelling make it an excellent way for organizations to engage more personally with their employees, achieving greater long-term loyalty and strengthening their corporate reputation. According to D'Ottavio (2020), storytelling is a growing trend "because brands are responding to consumers' need for storytelling with high quality content".

To craft a good story, you need:

- to think of a good storyline with a beginning, middle, and end. The beginning should grab people's attention and present relevant background information, providing a series of details to set the story in time and space. The middle of the story should lay out the obstacles and challenges that the organization and its representatives had to face. Finally, the story's outcome should be revealed at the end.
- a hero, a main character that the audience can relate to and admire. The story could also revolve around an antihero or villain that the audience wants to see defeated. Characters are the backbone of any good story. In this regard, identification is central to storytelling in PR. According to Kent (2015), "Identification happens when people believe they have something in common with someone or something else, or believe they are unlike someone or something else" (p. 483). In addition to having good characters, identification can be achieved by writing places or times that are familiar to the audience into the story.
- a memorable ending that pleases or surprises the audience. It can be happy or tragic and unexpected.

Following in the footsteps of Tobias (1993), Kent (2015) discusses some of the master plots that narratives can follow. These can be used by PR professionals to craft compelling stories. They include adventure, discovery, escape, forbidden love, love, maturation, metamorphosis, pursuit, quest, rescue, revenge, riddle/mystery, rise/fall, rivalry, sacrifice, temptation/greed, transformation, underdog, and wretched excess. A transformation plot might deal with a public figure who, after overcoming a serious illness, decides to make a radical change in their life or create a foundation aimed at helping others to overcome it as well. A story with an underdog plot, meanwhile, could feature an environmental activist who fights against big corporations and urges governments to protect the planet.

When constructing a narrative around an organization, we can draw on its history, telling stories about its beginnings and growth, its milestones, or the struggles it has had to face. We can also choose to focus on the organization itself and/or its founders, giving the stories an even more personal touch. We can tell stories to convey an organization's values as well. The featured character can embody these values, welcome audiences in, and connect with them on an emotional level.

Box 3.3

It all started with an air bed. Joe Gebbia, co-founder of Airbnb, gives a great example of storytelling in his TED talk (TED, 2016). "I want to tell you a story", he begins, before sharing how he struggled to pay rent every month as a young man. One day, he decided to put three air beds in his loft and rent them out as a bed and breakfast. Airbnb (a play on "air bed and breakfast") was born. Gebbia recounts all the challenges he had to overcome to become one of the most successful international start-ups of all time.

Box 3.4

"Love Them. Hate Them. Check Them". This campaign was run by Weber Shandwick for Breast Cancer Now, a breast cancer awareness charity that found many women had stopped going to the gynecologist because of COVID-19 (see WeberShandwick UK. (n.d.)). Partnering with filmmaker Anna Ginsburg, they created an animation film called *A Love/Hate Relationship* based on the real stories of women who had suffered from breast cancer. These women expressed a wide range of feelings about their experience, everywhere from pride to shame. By relaying these real-life stories, the film reached women on a more personal level.

3.3 Digitalization

Digitalization in corporate communication is growing at an unstoppable pace, as it is across every facet of society (medicine, education, etc.). The digital environment comes as an opportunity for PR firms to build and maintain relationships between organizations and their target consumers. This can be anything from creating content for organizations' websites and blogs to performing social media outreach on Twitter, Facebook, Instagram, TikTok, etc.

According to Baraybar (2007), the rise of social media has transformed how opinions are shaped and how information flows. Today's new technologies foster more individualized communication, making one-to-one interaction and creative strategies absolutely vital to successful communication. The author maintains that businesses and professionals can no longer hold the monopoly over information now that customers, stakeholders, and the public at large can share what they think about brands, products, and services. These communities have the power to shape society's opinions, forcing those in search of efficiency to blaze new trails, devise new strategies, and find forms of creativity that chime with the new social reality.

PR firms initially offered digital communication services separately from the other services in their catalog. Nowadays, its unthinkable to have a communication and PR project without a digital strategy to cultivate the organization's online presence so that it has a positive impact on its digital reputation. This online presence is now relying more and more on videos (shared via Reels, Live, etc.).

Today's ever-expanding digital world offers people more opportunities to consume informative and entertaining content. A significant part of the population has ceased to get the news from traditional media, turning instead to news aggregators such as Google News. As for entertainment, more and more consumers are choosing to watch content on digital platforms (Netflix, Disney+, HBO, etc.). All these shifts have had an impact on communication and PR strategies, which lean toward creating new content on organizations' owned media (e.g., their own newsletters and digital channels), earned media (digital media, comments by influencers, etc.), and shared media (digital environments where organizations and consumers can interact).

3.3.1 Banking on microinfluencers

Influencers are people who are popular on social media or other communication channels. Thanks to their authority, knowledge, or the relationship they have cultivated with their followers, the thoughts they share on specific topics can influence the attitudes and behavior of other people. Enke and Borchers (2019) define social media influencers as "third-party actors who have established a significant number of relevant relationships with a specific quality to and influence on organizational stakeholders through content production, content distribution, interaction, and personal appearance on the social web" (p. 261).

Once in the digital environment, it did not take brands and organizations long to realize how important it was to build good relationships with influencers. Today, these individuals continue to wield great power, although brands are choosing to partner more with microinfluencers. These are social media users who specialize in a niche market or specific area, share content about their interests through their accounts, and also publish sponsored posts when they partner with brands. They typically have between 1,000 and 3,000 followers and are valued by brands because their followers feel closer to them, seeing them more as peers. Microinfluencers tend to be more connected with their followers, replying to their comments and generating more engagement. It is more cost-effective for brands to collaborate with microinfluencers, as they can partner with several at the same time.

Box 3.5

Microinfluencers for a digital launch. The Lexus IS was launched digitally due to COVID-19 (like so many reveals) in June, 2020. Rather than casting actors, the campaign looked to appeal to potential owners by showing off the passions of eight microinfluencers, including a fashionista, a sneakerhead, a metalhead, an audiophile, a gamer, and a foodie, who became the centerpiece of every aspect of storytelling in the campaign (Bowman, 2021).

3.4 The rise of podcasts as a PR tool

Podcasts have boomed in recent years. According to data from Podcasthosting.org, in September, 2021, there were over two million podcasts and over 48 million episodes. Podcasts are on-demand audio files that can be listened to anywhere, at any time, on apps such as Apple Podcasts, Pocket Casts, and RadioPublic. They can also be downloaded onto mobile devices and listened to without an internet connection. What's more, people can listen to podcasts while on the move (e.g., while doing chores, jogging, or commuting to work), which opens up even more possibilities for when and where to listen to them. Because of what podcasts are, users can also share them on social media and thus increase their reach.

Podcasts can feature informative, educational, or entertaining content. In the beginning, because of their audio format, every radio program came to have their own podcast. Nowadays, however, there are many podcasts that have been created for specific purposes by different people, including organizational communication professionals. As Crawley (n.d.) says, "participating in a podcast gives the brand an opportunity to express its personality (and emotion) in a way that infographics, e-books and print interviews seldom do, because it's delivered in conversational language". Podcasts allow organizations to connect with their stakeholders more intimately, strengthening relationships in an audio environment.

Podcasts have given organizations a new way to communicate with their audiences (Scott, 2020). It is an owned medium (within the PESO model) that can be used to get messages across to audiences exactly as intended.

Although current technology can make it easy for organizations to record and edit podcasts themselves, they are better off ensuring quality sound production by recording in soundproof spaces, bringing in professional speakers and editors, etc. Poor technical quality can drive away the audience and negatively impact the organization's image. Organizations should also focus the content of their podcasts on topics that appeal to their target audiences. In other words, podcasts should not become broken-record advertisements about how amazing the products or services are. Instead, they should offer relevant content that sparks interest among those listening. Many podcasts created by businesses or institutions feature interviews with their top executives, experts, or invited guests, which makes for a varied selection of content and can position the organization as an expert in a given area, thereby strengthening its credibility. In this regard, according to Edelman's 2021 Trust Barometer, businesses are some of the most trusted institutions worldwide.

Podcasting requires the involvement of an organization's executives; they need to look and feel comfortable sharing their ideas and opinions publicly. If the decision is made to post new podcasts every so often, an effort needs to be made to come up with content on time, as listeners value consistency.

While many corporate podcasts target external audiences, organizations can also produce internal podcasts, creating content that their employees can listen to while they are at or away from work to boost their engagement.

Finally, podcasts should align with the organization's communication plan and be shared across all available channels, including social media.

Box 3.6

"**#Lipstories**" is a series of podcasts created by Girlboss Radio in partnership with Sephora. Each episode features an influential woman who tells her own story, addressing topics such as self-esteem and body positivity. According to the podcast's description, "Guests recount their favorite memories – from childhood to today – where they felt beautiful, powerful, or like their best selves" (Girlboss Radio. Apple Podcasts).

As Williams (2020) mentioned, "on the surface, podcasting might seem like an awkward fit for a beauty brand. It's obviously not a visual medium, and podcast listenership as a whole tends to skew male. But with a focus on empowering and inspiring listeners with honest and engaging storytelling, the "#Lipstories" podcast perfectly complements the lipstick line's tagline—"lipstick for real life"—and helps to establish its authenticity in the minds of listeners".

3.5 Online and hybrid events

Many events were thrust online due to the COVID-19 pandemic. However, the PR industry was already leaning into a number of technological advancements before it hit, for example using social media to promote events and establish two-way communication with attendees, streaming content, developing event-specific apps, using big data, and harnessing the Internet of Things and artificial intelligence.

There are several factors that have made it easier to move events online. These include heightened digital literacy among the population and the ease with which younger generations—such as Gen Z—interact and socialize in online environments; society's demand for more sustainable events, above all considering the huge environmental impact made by those traveling internationally; and the level of technological advancement in devices and the 5G network, as well as the growing number of people who own these devices and have internet at home.

Some of the advantages of online events are ease of attendance, lower costs, the ability to reach wider audiences, greater long-term availability of the content, and reduced carbon emissions due to less travel. However, there is consensus in the sector that certain types of events are more difficult to move online than others. Conferences, congresses, and even product presentations have a longer track record online (just think of webinars and virtual congresses, for example). In contrast, there are certain types of events whose move online is not yet feasible.

While the COVID-19 lockdown was in place, many efforts were made to organize meetings via Zoom, Webex, Google Meet, etc. While these tools do enable many people to connect at the same time, the meetings they facilitate are not really online events. Organizing an online event requires a specific strategic design that factors in the attendees' physical absence and provides spaces for interaction.

Online events take place entirely on websites rather than at real-life venues. Following are 15 points to bear in mind when designing an online event:

(1) Design the event specifically for it to take place in an online environment. That means not attempting to copy the same dynamics used at in-person events, but rather adapting the program to the new context.

(2) Look into who is coming to the event and consider how adept they might be at using the latest technologies. Use the tools that best suit them. What's important is that the content be easily accessible. Make sure to provide information on how the online venue works in advance and set up a support channel to field issues during the event.

(3) Create a visually appealing website for the event that works on all devices (PCs, tablets, and smartphones).

(4) Create a specific app for the event that displays everything people need to know about it and provides instant access.

(5) Make sure the online venue is user-friendly. It should be convenient, intuitive, and easy to browse.

(6) Upload content before the event begins (schedule, infographics, materials, presentation videos, etc.)

(7) Create a visually pleasing invitation and registration system that provides details about the event.

(8) Set up spaces for attendees to interact. Beyond the more formal channels for sending in questions (with the recommended moderator figure), it is important to have spaces that foster social interaction and networking and that allow attendees to engage in informal chats.

(9) Design an attractive venue. Getting the setting right has always been key for event organizers, who often lean into a certain theme. This is essential for online events as well. The venue should reflect the values of the organizer and its collaborators and sponsors.

(10) Design an environment using virtual or augmented reality. Virtually recreating a real-life place to host an event can help attendees feel more immersed in the experience. It is a matter of harnessing the same technology that is already widely used in virtual tours of museums and other cultural centers. You can also design and create made-up places specifically for the event. What's most important is that the attendees can interact with their surroundings and virtually move about them. Virtual reality technology is advancing rapidly and, although it was once used mainly in entertainment (e.g., for videogames), it has now been adapted for event organization.

(11) Give people avatars (i.e., graphic figures of them). To enhance the feeling of immersion, every attendee could have their own avatar. Today's technology makes it possible to create avatars that accurately match people's physical appearance. People's avatars can then interact in the various spaces designed for the event

(12) Use storytelling. This is a communication technique that has been used in PR and corporate communication campaigns for years. It has potential in online event organization as well, conveying messages to attendees through stories and appealing more to their emotions. Storytelling can give the event a common thread and help get more engagement out of those attending.

(13) Encourage attendee participation. One option is to gamify the event, which means coming up with games, contests, or other fun ways to incentivize the attendees' engagement and involvement.

(14) Promote the event on social media. Social media can be used to high-light the event before, during, and after. It is important to maintain ongoing interaction with everyone involved.

(15) Keep the event content available. Record the event so that those inter-ested can watch it afterwards. This is a good way to further its reach.

Box 3.7

#GlobalPrideCrossing was a virtual Global Pride event held in the video game *Animal Crossing*. Pride month—a celebration of values such as equality, dignity, visibility, and self-love—lost its momentum at a key time of the year due to the global pandemic. With hundreds of live events cancelled, millions of members of the LGBTQI+ com-munity lost out on the chance to gather, celebrate their identity, and fight for their rights.

As Iucksch et al. (2020) pointed out, "according to LGBTI+ mem-bers, the social aspect of Pride was the biggest casualty. This led to a major channel insight: the best platform to host the activation was not a social network, but a social game. And the "gaymers" community had a new favorite venue: *Animal Crossing: New Horizons*".

The event was set on a customized Pride-themed island, with typi-cal Pride features such as a rainbow-colored brick crossing, a Queer Hall of Fame, a custom clothing collection, and much more. Influenc-ers were also involved and LGBTQI+ communities from around the world were invited to join in (We Are Social, n.d.).

Halfway between in-person and online events, there is a third option: the **hybrid event**. This type of event takes place at a real-life venue but can also be attended online. Thanks to this type of setup, as with online events, you can:

- reach wider audiences by not forcing people to travel to a specific place to attend;
- achieve greater sustainability;
- lower costs;
- track the attendees' behavior more accurately and get real-time feed-back; and
- make the content available for longer by recording it and putting it up online, which translates to a greater overall reach down the line.

Hybrid events, unlike online events, take place partly in-person. The speakers, and even some of the attendees, may be in one place (or several places), while everyone else joins in online. The in-person activity is usually carried out at a venue designed to resemble a television set and is live streamed for those at home. However, a hybrid event is not the same as a simple live stream. Hybrid events must be custom-designed with this setup in mind, leveraging the best of both in-person and online events. Whatever the case, organizers will need to tap into their creativity and ensure good video production (script, storytelling, host, set, cameras, lighting, music, etc.).

One of the most important aspects to consider when organizing a hybrid event is interattendee activity. This means not making the mistake of focusing everyone's attention solely on what is going on at the in-person venue and thus treating the online attendees like mere spectators. The goal is to ensure that everyone feels equally seen, heard, and involved in the event, thereby achieving a great level of engagement all around.

Event organizers can use new developments in technology to bridge the gap between in-person and online environments. Until now, online and hybrid events have struggled most notably to enable the type of informal interactions that naturally occur at in-person events (networking, coffee breaks, etc.). To overcome this, organizers can use tools to foster such interaction as well as create high-quality content to offer a meaningful immersive experience to everyone attending. As the attention span of online attendees is much shorter (they are only one click away from leaving the event), the duration and pace of the event become determining factors.

Following are some key points for livening up hybrid events:

- choose an eye-catching venue that is set up specifically for live-streaming and pair it with an immersive online environment;
- pay attention to the event's look, giving it a distinct visual identity;
- find a host that has what it takes to enliven the event and encourage the attendees to participate;
- keep the attendees' expectations high by proposing votes, contests, and interactive polls whose results can be seen and shared during the event;
- plan fun activities and use gamification techniques that let people see how they ranked and who the prize-winners are;
- how about real-time coffee breaks and toasts? Before the event takes place, send a specially prepared kit to each attendee's home in custom packaging that features the event's image. Invite everyone to enjoy what's inside during the event;
- work with specific online platforms that allow the attendees to interact (putting anyone who expressed similar interests at registration in contact, for instance);

- personalize the experience. If it is an international congress, for example, personalize the event program to match each attendee's time zone, session preferences, etc.;
- up the entertainment factor by including activities that break the ice, lighten the mood, and keep the event upbeat. These could include musical performances, escape rooms, team-building activities, or wellness workshops that help prevent the side effects of sitting for too long and watching the event through a screen.

Box 3.8

A launching event in an online format. Apple's new product launches always create a lot of buzz and are usually hybrid. The 2020 Apple Worldwide Developers Conference, however, took place entirely online, featuring a keynote speech and sessions that connected millions of developers across the globe (Apple, 2020). The production value was exceptional: Apple used the latest audio and video techniques and had well-thought-out transitions that gave extra oomph to the event. With CEO Tim Cook on stage and the audience watching at home, Apple set a new benchmark for hybrid and online events.

3.6 Brand and organizational communication in the metaverse

Described as the "new chapter" of the Internet, the metaverse is a virtual world where people connect using 3D glasses and later with more advanced, lightweight virtual, and augmented reality devices. In this new universe, each person will have their own avatar—with characteristics similar, or not, to their physical features—that, through sensors, can replicate the movement of the person and interact with other people. Its promoters also announce that the metaverse will allow for the creation of totally personalized spaces in which avatars will be able to work, shop, meet, and carry out all kinds of activities.

The functionalities of the metaverse are where communication professionals can think about the possibilities for organizing marketing, advertising, or PR campaigns, including different types of events for different brands, companies, and organizations. We have already seen the emergence of practices such as advergaming and in-game advertising in such virtual environments as video games, as well as concerts and other events staged virtually. Various spaces of this new virtual environment are emerging in the metaverse, and in the future, they will offer multiple and diverse settings in which to interact and host virtual interactive events.

3.7 The impact of COVID-19 on public relations

COVID-19 hit the PR industry hard, forcing people to work from home and adjust their yearly communication plans while in lockdown. The pandemic made creativity more essential than ever in PR for finding new ways to communicate with organizations' stakeholders. The new landscape also prompted areas of specialization such as crisis and risk communication, internal communication, CSR, and online event organization.

While most workers, children, and entire families were in lockdown, many companies devised PR actions aimed specifically at people stuck at home. Their messages took on a more emotional, empathetic tone, many brands shifted their narrative (recalling their values and history and sending messages of hope and encouragement), and many companies also carried out actions to support healthcare professionals, for example.

Box 3.9

In 2020, Whirlpool's brand mission to foster "**Every Day, Care**" took on new meaning when families were stuck at home under stay-at-home orders. To help parents through this challenging time, Whirlpool, with support from Ketchum, worked to turn chores into fun ways for children to learn basic skills and self-reliance (Ketchum, n.d.). The company partnered with a handful of influencers, including Sean Lowe, the popular star of *The Bachelor* and father of three. To amplify the campaign, Whirlpool arranged local interviews with home organization expert Brooke Parkhurst, who highlighted the importance of teaching valuable life lessons through chores. These fun chore exercises were also shared on the brand's social media and Whirlpool.com to increase reach.

Box 3.10

Over 1,000 businesses, organizations, and institutions across 34 countries joined the Spanish creative boutique Shackleton's

"**#The200Challenge**" initiative by temporarily changing their logos to raise awareness about the importance of keeping a safe personal distance of at least 200 cm from others and preventing the spread of coronavirus. Brands such as Decathlon, Coca-Cola, Audi, L'Oreal, and Zara took part. The last of these changed its logo by adding the slogan "Respecting social distancing but staying closer than ever".

The healthcare crisis triggered by the pandemic, as well as its many other consequences, prompted the PR sector to bolster areas such as:

- **Crisis and risk communication**: PR managers began to roll out crisis communication plans and require specialized PR services to deal with the new situation from a communication standpoint. This area proved crucial and will continue to be developed to face uncertain scenarios in the future.

Box 3.11

Inoue PR created the **"COVID-19 Rapid Response Communications Manual"** in April 2020 in the midst of the global spread of the COVID-19 pandemic. It has since been provided free of charge to more than 1,100 companies and local governments in Japan. The downloaded manual enables them to draft their own response policies as well as to improve communications internally and externally. The manual outlines the basic concepts and procedures for these organizations to collect and disseminate relevant information from a crisis management perspective.

- **Internal communication:** It became critical and needed to be adapted to the fact that many were working from home. It had to become mobile-first and overcome the challenge of fostering a sense of connectedness and cohesion among employees. Internal communication will continue to be crucial for organizations when it comes to retaining and attracting talent in the future.

- **CSR** and the purpose of organizations became key issues, as society began to expect organizations to cooperate in combating the pandemic. The demand for social contribution is set to grow in the future as well.

The "Companies in the post-COVID-19 world" report produced by Corporate Excellence—Centre for Reputation Leadership in alliance with Kirishu (March 2021), shows a strengthened correlation between purpose and reputation. Companies with a defined and active purpose report an 83% improvement in reputation among employees, 69.5% among customers, 52% among society, 44% among suppliers, and 42% among shareholders and investors. According to the report's findings, the new COVID-19 habitat places value on the role of purpose-driven companies, which goes beyond shareholder return, recognizing those that are capable of understanding social expectations and demands, while at the same time presenting appropriate solutions and behaviors.

Box 3.12

The importance of mental health became apparent during the COVID-19 crisis. Instagram set out to help people cope with the adverse effects of home-isolation and COVID-19 by shining a light on mental well-being and opening up avenues of communication about it. Together with Archetype and Spain's Mental Health Confederation, it created the first **Instagram Guides** in Spain. By enlisting the help of health professionals, illustrators, and public figures, the social network aimed to become a source of reliable, high-quality content (Raya, 2021).

Box 3.13

"We can't move forward until we can all move forward". In a public statement, Uber wrote, "Transportation shouldn't be a barrier to vaccination; however, 6 million people miss medical appointments because they don't have a ride" (Uber, 2021). The mobility-as-a-service company ended up donating 10 million rides in the US to help those most in need. Lyft also offered free rides to vaccination centers in the US. Meanwhile, President Biden announced an agreement with the companies as part of the country's efforts to vaccinate 70% of the population before Independence Day.

- **Online events**: Between lockdowns and stay-at-home orders, it was impossible to hold in-person events, and the economic fallout was devastating for the MICE industry. Online events eased the industry out of stagnation while also fast-tracking digitalization processes.

Box 3.13

"**Colours of Carnival**". In 2020, Samsung Electronics UK harnessed its technology to broadcast the Notting Hill Carnival online during the pandemic, shooting videos in 8K on the Samsung Galaxy S20. "The films celebrated Carnival by shining a spotlight on the festival's vibrancy and energy through dance, food and music" (Samsung Newsroom UK, 2020). Organized by Taylor Herring, the event won the Best PR Event award at the 2021 PRWeek Awards.

Box 3.14

"**One World: Together at Home**", organized by Pepsi and Global Citizen, was a special program broadcast worldwide on television and online in April, 2020, to support those on the frontline against COVID-19 and to raise funds to help combat the pandemic. The concert was endorsed by the World Health Organization (WHO) (see World Health Organization-WHO, 2020), which announced it at a joint press conference with Lady Gaga. The broadcast featured artists such as Alanis Morissette, Andrea Bocelli, Billie Eilish, Chris Martin, Elton John, Paul McCartney, and Stevie Wonder, who did not perform on stage but rather at their homes. In addition to the musical talent, several of the world's leading personalities also made an appearance, including the Beckhams, Ellen DeGeneres, Heidi Klum, Lewis Hamilton, and Samuel L. Jackson (World Health Organization, 2020).

- **PR creativity itself:**
  According to the *2021 Creativity In PR* study, 55% of respondents said the pandemic helped their agency's creative game, while 31% described it as neutral, and only 12% as negative (PRovoke & Now Go Create, 2021). As a matter of fact, data from this study indicates

that "more than a half of agencies (56%) report they are more likely to be approached for big, creative ideas than they were 12 months ago" (p. 20). In this regard, Dan Margulis, executive creative director of FleishmanHillard, observes that "so many in our industry are stronger, smarter, braver, and better built to reshape the future. Crisis forced us to act but also freed us to evolve. We didn't get there through convention. We have creativity to thank for getting us through" (PRovoke & Now Go Create, 2021, p. 7). Likewise, Claire Bridges, the founder of Now Go Create and coauthor of the *2021 Creativity In PR* study says, "from a purely creative point of view, the pandemic has clearly presented PR with an opportunity to experiment and consider new ways to do things we took for granted" (Sudhaman, 2021).

The results of this study also indicate that creativity is a very important factor for the recovery of the PR sector after the COVID pandemic (88% of respondents) and that clients' expectations of creativity have increased since the outbreak (92%).

3.8 The importance of internal communication

In today's (pre and postpandemic) world, shaped by globalization and the rise of new digital technologies, organizations must be adaptive. Plus, many companies' main asset is the talent of their employees, which proves vital to their operation and their ability to reach their goals and objectives.

Internal communication is one of the key components of successful communication plans in organizations. Despite focusing almost exclusively on communicating with their customers in the past, companies and institutions today are increasingly tuned in to the importance of maintaining ongoing communication with their employees as well. A good internal communication policy makes it possible to effectively convey an organization's mission, vision, and values. It also creates a positive work environment and boosts employee motivation, making it easier to attract and retain talent and to foster employees' feeling of unity, team spirit, and belonging. Employees who are happy with the way they are treated by their company and who are proud of the way it behaves will speak well of it outside working hours, which will help to improve its reputation and attract new talent.

An organization's internal communication strategy must be developed in conjunction with its human resources team and address both vertical communication (top-down and bottom-up, between management and employees) and horizontal communication (between employees at the same level).

Internal communication often takes place via an intranet, a newsletter, or social media. Other traditional channels include noticeboards, information displays, suggestion boxes, and emails. It is important to have two-way channels set up so that employees can actively be heard; an internal chat is good for this. Organizations can also try out new communication channels (e.g., apps), use data analytics to tailor content, or employ storytelling techniques.

To improve internal communication, you should:

- conduct workplace climate surveys so that every employee has a way to voice their opinion and offer suggestions. This type of survey makes it possible to detect faults and errors before they get out of hand, so that solutions can be drawn up in time;
- be transparent toward your internal audiences, communicating any circumstances, developments, or changes that affect the organization;
- hold more effective, productive, and inspiring meetings, especially when they take place online. Many employees dislike meetings, usually because they are too long or because they are used to communicate information one-directionally (top-down) when this could be better handled through other channels, such as an email or one-on-one conversation. Other times, this is because they are held on a regular basis whether or not they are really necessary or because it is unclear what everyone attending is expected to contribute. Before calling a meeting, make sure you know what it is for and what you hope to achieve by the time it ends. You must let people know in advance what is on the agenda, how long the meeting is set to last, and what they should do to prepare for it (i.e., what tasks they should complete beforehand to make sure the meeting is productive). Furthermore, meetings should only be attended by key people, so that no one feels dispensable, and they should not become overly crowded. The key is to only invite people who absolutely need to be there, that is, who have something to contribute, who have something to gain by attending, or who are directly affected by the outcome. Punctuality and timing are also essential; start and end meetings as scheduled and keep them under the recommended 50 minutes. It is also important to foster a safe, inclusive atmosphere where everyone feels free to share their ideas without fear of criticism or indifference. This is vital for creativity to flow. Make sure everyone has the chance to get a word in. The conversation should not be monopolized by only a few people. More active participation can also be achieved by asking people to avoid multitasking, as this lowers performance and stifles creative potential. Online meetings can use all the resources offered by platforms and be coordinated by moderators: chats, polls, whiteboards, screen-sharing, and so on. Another option is to put people in smaller breakout groups before joining everyone back up. To keep the meeting engaging, you can use techniques

such as those described in Chapter 2: brainstorming, six thinking hats, mind mapping, etc. Someone should be tasked with taking notes during the meeting and then later typing up the minutes. This task cannot be done by the person leading the meeting. The last few minutes of the meeting should be used to go over who is in charge of doing what and by when. After the meeting, the organizer should send the minutes—including decisions, actions, and any relevant materials—to everyone who attended and then follow up on the actions on the agreed days. You can also make meetings more effective by putting some creativity into where it is held, how the space is set up, etc.;

- invest in actions aimed at improving employees' physical, psychological, and social well-being, such as activities that foster healthy lifestyle habits (nutrition, exercise, etc.), showing the utmost regard for employees and their health. Corporate wellness policies will also help boost employees' creativity. Indeed, studies such as Oppezzo and Schwartz (2014) have linked exercise (e.g., going for short walks) to improved creativity;
- organize events for employees somewhere exiting and new that takes them away from the workplace. These could be welcome events for new employees, farewell parties for those retiring, Christmas dinners, open days for family members, celebrations for a certain number of years served, employee sporting events, company anniversaries, and so on. All of them can be designed with a high dose of creativity;
- apply gamification techniques that boost engagement through prizes and rewards;
- organize team-building activities to increase trust between team members, nurture a positive working environment, and boost productivity in the organization. Sporting, volunteering, cultural, or other activities can relieve tensions and bring the team together toward a common goal.

Box 3.15

As Harrington (2020) highlighted, "AXA Health chief executive Tracy Garrad joined TV presenter Gabby Logan on a **'COVID-tested road trip'** to some of AXA Health's locations, to meet its people and learn about its newest innovations". Employees were able to share questions, experiences, and proposals for improvement with her, which were subsequently displayed on the company's intranet and other internal communication channels, and some of the suggested initiatives were developed.

Box 3.16

#AVIDAEMNOSSASMÃOS. In September 2018, a workplace accident occurred at a DSM Nutritional Products factory in Brazil. The company realized that its workers had not fully assimilated its Life-Saving Rules. With the help of Ideal H+K Strategies, an internal communication campaign was launched to increase awareness of the importance of following these rules. Within 10 months, the accident rate had dropped.

3.9 Purpose-driven organizations and CSR

According to the Friedman Doctrine, which is named after the well-known American economist Milton Friedman, "the one and only social purpose of business is to increase its profits". Profitability is indeed essential; without it, companies cannot pursue other goals or become sustainable in the long term. However, money aside, today's companies must also be accountable to society for the impact their actions have on the population and the environment.

In a world as globalized as today's, where every employee and supplier has the means to publicly praise or criticize their employer (e.g., using social media to post about something instantaneously), companies must behave within society's expectations and effectively communicate their CSR actions, which in turn should line up with their values. Growing awareness of environmental degradation and the legislative impetus exerted by public bodies are forcing companies to act more sustainably. Those that do also enjoy a better reputation. In fact, according to Virakul et al. (2009), improving reputation is one of the reasons that companies give for being more socially responsible, although this cannot become a masquerade, an act of greenwashing (misleading the public with regard to a company's environmental practices or the environmental benefits of a product or service), or a one-off philanthropic venture. The commitment needs to be genuine, as reputation implies acting ethically, ensuring consistency between what is said and done, and demonstrating transparency in this respect. A company that works under sustainability principles must integrate these principles into its organizational culture, something that is done by purpose-driven organizations, as stated by Henderson and Van den Steen (2015).

According to Yadav (2021), "in 2021 and beyond, PR professionals will have to guide organizations to exhibit authenticity, communicate their values and demonstrate how they add to the advancement of society".

Purpose-driven companies are more appealing when it comes to recruiting and retaining talent and are more attractive to customers. According to O'Brien et al. (2019), "purpose-driven companies witness higher market share gains and grow three times faster on average than their competitors, all while achieving higher workforce and customer satisfaction". In fact, according to another study conducted in 2020, consumers are six times more likely to buy products and use services from brands and companies with a strong purpose (Zeno Group, 2020). Similar data were provided by the Purpose Perception study, which found that lead-with-purpose companies are 78% more attractive to work for and 76% more trusted by consumers (Porter Novelli, 2021). In addition, 75% of respondents said they remembered companies with a strong purpose more. According to the study's overall findings, when brands are purposeful, they connect with consumers on an emotional level that transcends their functional attributes. A company's purpose also makes it more identifiable and gives it differential value, underlining its *raison d'être*. Communicating a company's purpose allows it to create deeper connections with its stakeholders.

Vredenburg et al. (2020) explore another aspect linked to brand purpose: corporate activism. For these authors, many consumers now expect brands and organizations to take a strong stance on sociopolitical issues that affect citizens.

PR helps to create and distribute content about the purpose, values, and CSR actions of organizations. This commitment to society must not only be communicated outwardly, however. Organizations must act accordingly and have a good internal communication plan to involve their employees in their corporate values.

The Sustainable Development Goals (SDGs) set out in the 2030 Agenda, promoted by the United Nations and adopted by its Member States in 2015, have also helped to place CSR at the core of many companies' management, and this is relayed to stakeholders through communication and PR actions.

Box 3.17

To shine a light on people over the age of 65 who experience unwanted loneliness, the BBK Foundation, which is run by Basque Bank Bilbao Bizkai Kutxa, launched a project called "Invisible soledad" (**Invisible loneliness**) with the help of communication and PR firm LLYC. A hyper-realistic sculpture of Mercedes, an 88-year-old woman from Bilbao who has suffered loneliness in this way for years, was installed at one of the busiest points in Bilbao. It represented the waiting that many people endure in solitude. After two days, with the public's eye on the sculpture, it was revealed that Mercedes, the person who inspired it, was real and alive. The project managed to demonstrate that the worst thing about loneliness is not death itself, but the road to it (BBK Foundation, n.d.).

Box 3.18

From Golin agency comments that "**Colors of the World**" where launched by Crayola introducing "24 new specially formulated crayons designed to represent over 40 global skin tones so children could accurately color themselves into the world . . . to increase representation and foster a greater sense of inclusion" (Golin, n.d.-a). With the help of another agency, Dentsu, they also created the **"Draw your #TrueSelfie"** campaign, using the colors of the world crayons to build self-esteem and self-confidence in kids, creating an online gallery. The campaign was an instant success, with thousands of media features and social media influencer support across the web (Dentsu, n.d.).

3.9.1 Sustainability

Among the 17 Sustainable Development Goals (SDGs), there are some specifically focused on environmental protection, such as those that call to "take urgent action to combat climate change and its impacts" (SDG 13), "conserve and sustainably use the oceans, seas and marine resources for sustainable development" (SDG 14), and "protect, restore and promote sustainable use of terrestrial ecosystems, sustainably manage forests, combat desertification, and halt and reverse land degradation and halt biodiversity loss" (SDG 15).

Governments are campaigning to get people to embrace environmental values. Environmental communication seeks to promote environmental literacy. Applied to organizations, it requires transparent and frank disclosure of their environmental activities and impacts. An increasing number of organizations are integrating their environmental communication and producing environmental reports, which can be included in the general annual report or drawn up separately.

One of the major issues facing the world is climate change. The activities of multinationals and large consumer companies have a huge impact on the environment. However, there are also companies that are committed to reducing their environmental footprint, companies which recycle, reforest, save energy, lower their water consumption, reduce their CO_2 emissions, etc.

As Buil and Roger (2014) point out, the environment is present across all areas of society, but fostering respectful attitudes toward the environment is not easy, and requires specialized communication that includes specific strategies and techniques that not only impart knowledge, but also raise awareness and achieve the desired environmental behavior. This is where environmental communication comes into play in companies, public bodies, social organizations, the media, and social networks, through social responsibility campaigns, communication strategies, environmental management models, community action programs, and so on.

Box 3.19

"Treeless world". To raise awareness about deforestation, the World Wildlife Fund produced a film set in what seemed to be a typical Fortnite landscape, except without any trees, which are players' main source of protection in the game. The campaign, whose message was "If we miss nature in a game, imagine it in the real world", was developed by AlmaBBDO and won a Young Lions Live Award at the Cannes Lions International Festival of Creativity (Oréfice, 2021).

References

Apple (2020, March 13). *La Conferencia Mundial de Desarrolladores de Apple 2020 arranca en junio con un nuevo formato online.* www.apple.com/es/newsroom/2020/03/apples-wwdc-2020-kicks-off-in-june-with-an-all-new-online-format/

Bagozzi, R. P., Gopinath, M., & Nyer, P. U. (1999). The role of emotions in marketing. *Journal of the Academy of Marketing Science, 27*(2), 184–206.

Baraybar, A. (2007). La innovación en las empresas de comunicación y relaciones públicas en la cultura 2.0. *Creatividad y Sociedad, 11*, 106.

BBK Foundation. (n.d.). *Invisible soledad.* https://invisiblesoledad.com

Boje, D. (2008). *Storytelling organizations.* SAGE.

Bowman, J. (2021, August). How micro-influencers helped drive sales of the Lexus IS. *WARC.* www.warc.com

Buil, P., & Roger, O. (2014). Manual de comunicación ambiental: del greenwashing a la sostenibilidad. *Manual de comunicación ambiental*, 1–200.

Chóliz, M. (2005). *Psicología de la emoción: el proceso emocional.* www.uv.es/~choliz/Procesoemocional.pdf

Crawley, M. (n.d.). *4 Tips for using a podcast as a PR tool.* https://tricomb2b.com/resources/blog/4-tips-using-podcast-pr-tool

Dentsu. (n.d.). *Crayola Color Your World*. www.dentsu.com/us/en/our-work/crayola-color-your-world

D'Ottavio, D. (2020, June 29). In 2020 and beyond, earned media should take priority. *PR Daily*. www.prdaily.com/in-2020-and-beyond-earned-media-should-take-priority/

Edelman. (2021). *Edelman's Trust barometer 2021*. www.edelman.com/trust/2021-trust-barometer

Elmer, P. (2016). Public relations and storytelling. In L. Edwards & C. E. M. Hodges (Eds.), Public relations, *society and culture*. Theoretical and empirical explorations (pp. 47–60). Routledge.

Enke, N., & Borchers, N. S. (2019). Social media influencers in strategic communication: A conceptual framework for strategic social media influencer communication. *International Journal of Strategic Communication, 13*(4), 261–277.

Eurobest. (2019). *Choose your future*. https://www2.eurobest.com/winners/2019/media/entry.cfm?entryid=1316&award=101&order=2&direction=1

Eysenck, M. W. (1982). *Attention and arousal: Cognition and performance*. Springer-Verlag.

Ferreras, A. P. (1995). *Psicología Básica: introducción al estudio de la conducta humana*. Pirámide.

Fundación BBK. (n.d.). *Invisible soledad*. https://invisiblesoledad.com

Gill, R. (2011). Corporate storytelling as an effective internal public relations strategy. *International Business and Management, 3*(1), 17–25.

Girlboss Radio. Lipstories (n.d.). *Apple Podcasts*. https://podcasts.apple.com/es/podcast/lipstories/id1370728732

Goleman, D. (1999). *Inteligencia emocional*. Kairós.

Golin (n.d.-a). *Crayola: Colors of the world*. https://golin.com/work/crayola-colors-of-the-world/

Golin (n.d.-b). *Dove: Project #ShowUs*. https://golin.com/emea/work/dove-project-showus/

Greenspan, S. I. (1997). *The growth of the mind: And the endangered origins of intelligence*. Addison-Wesley.

Harrington, J. (2020, October 28). Watch: Jack Whitehall gets fit from everyday activities for AXA Health. *PR Week*. www.prweek.com/article/1698594/watch-jack-whitehall-gets-fit-everyday-activities-axa-health

Heath, R. L. (2000). A rhetorical perspective on the values of public relations: Crossroads and pathways toward concurrence. *Journal of Public Relations Research, 12*(1), 69–91.

Henderson, R., & Van den Steen, E. (2015). Why do firms have" purpose"? The firm's role as a carrier of identity and reputation. *American Economic Review, 105*(5), 326–330.

Iucksch, W., Tan, M., & Robin, A. (2020). Global pride: Global pride crossing. *WARC Media Awards, Silver, Effective Use of Tech*. www.warc.com

Jin, Y. (2010). Emotional leadership as a key dimension of public relations leadership: A national survey of public relations leaders. *Journal of Public Relations Research, 22*(2), 159–181.

Kent, M. L. (2015). The power of storytelling in public relations: Introducing the 20 master plots. *Public Relations Review, 41*(4), 480–489.

Ketchum (n.d.). *Whirlpool: Chore club.* www.ketchum.com/work/whirlpool-chore-club/

LeDoux, J. E. (2000). Emotion circuits in the brain. *Annual Review of Neuroscience, 23*(1), 155–184.

L'Etang, J. (2009). *Relaciones públicas: Conceptos, práctica y crítica.* Editorial UOC.

Mayer, J. D., Salovey, P., & Caruso, D. R. (2004). Emotional intelligence: Theory, findings, and implications. *Psychological Inquiry. An International Journal for the Advancement of Psychological Theory, 15*(3), 197–215.

O'Brien, D., Main, A., Kounkel, S., & Stephan, A. R. (2019). Purpose is everything. How brands that authentically lead with purpose are changing the nature of business today. *Deloitte.* https://www2.deloitte.com/us/en/insights/topics/marketing-and-sales-operations/global-marketing-trends/2020/purpose-driven-companies.html

Oppezzo, M., & Schwartz, D. L. (2014). Give your ideas some legs: The positive effect of walking on creative thinking. *Journal of Experimental Psychology: Learning, Memory, and Cognition, 40*(4), 1142.

Oréfice, G. (2021, April 4). Dupla brasileira é premiada no Young Lions. *Meio e Mensagem.* www.meioemensagem.com.br/home/comunicacao/2021/04/26/dupla-brasileira-e-premiada-no-cannes-lions.html

Patti, C. H., & Moriarty, S. E. (1990). *The making of effective advertising.* Prentice Hall.

Payne, W. L. (1985). *A study of emotion: Developing Emotional Intelligence; Self-Integration; Relating to Fear, Pain and Desire* (*Theory, Structure of Reality, Problem-Solving, Contraction/Expansion, Tuning In/Coming Out/Letting Go*) (Doctoral dissertation). Union for Experimenting Colleges and Universities. http://eqi.org/payne.htm

Plutchik, R. (1980). *Emotion: A psychoevolutionary synthesis.* Harper & Row.

Podcasthosting.org. (2021, September). *2021 Global podcast statistics, demographics & habits.* https://podcasthosting.org/podcast-statistics/

Porter Novelli. (2021). *Purpose perception.* www.porternovelli.com/findings/purpose-perception-porter-novellis-implicit-association-study/

PRovoke Media & Now Go Create. (2021). *Creativity in PR 2021 Global Study.* PRovoke. https://www.provokemedia.com/ranking-and-data/creativity-in-pr

Raya, L. (2021, January 5). Crear unas 'guías' como eje de una estrategia debranded content. *Top Comunicacion.* www.topcomunicacion.com/crear-guias-utiles-branded-content/

Reeve, J. (2010). *Motivación y emoción.* McGraw-Hill.

Samsung Newsroom UK. (2020, August 19). *Company info | about us |Samsung UK.* www.samsung.com/uk/about-us/company-info/

Scott, D. M. (2020). *The new rules of marketing and PR: How to use content marketing, podcasting, social media, AI, live video, and newsjacking to reach buyers directly.* John Wiley & Sons.

Sudhaman, A. (2021, June 21). 2021 Study: PR industry rises to covid-era creative challenge. *Provoke.* www.provokemedia.com/long-reads/article/2021-study-pr-industry-rises-to-covid-era-creative-challenge

TED. (2016, February). *Joe Gebbia*. www.ted.com/talks/joe_gebbia_how_airbnb_designs_for_trust

Tobias, R. B. (1993). *20 master plots (and how to build them)*. Writer's Digest Books.

Uber. (2021). *We can't move forward until we can all move forward – COVID-19 resources*. www.uber.com/us/en/coronavirus/

Virakul, B., Koonmee, K., & McLean, G. N. (2009). CSR activities in award-winning Thai companies. *Social Responsibility Journal, 5*(2), 178–199. https://doi.org/10.1108/17471110910964478

Vredenburg, J., Kapitan, S., Spry, A., & Kemper, J. A. (2020). Brands taking a stand: Authentic brand activism or woke washing? *Journal of Public Policy & Marketing, 39*(4), 444–460.

We Are Social. (n.d.). *Global pride crossing*. https://wearesocial.com/es/case-study/global-pride-crossing/

Weber Shandwick UK. (n.d.). *Breast cancer now. A love-hate relationship*. https://webershandwick.co.uk/our-work/breast-cancer-now-a-love-hate-relationship/

Williams, R. (2020, January 2). 10 companies doing branded podcasts the right way. *The Slice*. https://theslice.thecontentdivision.com.au/case-studies/10-companies-doing-branded-podcasts-the-right-way/

World Health Organization (WHO). (2020, April 6). El movimiento internacional Global Citizen y la OMS anuncian la realización de One World: Together At Home, un programa especial que se transmitirá a todo el mundo por televisión e internet en apoyo de quienes luchan contra la pandemia de COVID-19.

Yadav, P. (2021). 3 Upcoming trends in public relations. *PR Intelligence Online*. www.printelligenceonline.com/3-upcoming-trends-in-public-relations/

Zeitlin, D. M., & Westwood, R. A. (1986). Measuring emotional response. *Journal of Advertising Research, 26*(5), 34–44.

Zeno Group (2020, June 17). *The 2020 Zeno strength of purpose study*. www.zenogroup.com/insights/2020-zeno-strength-purpose

4   The public relations sector among the creative industries

4.1 Creative industries and the future of economy

In the postindustrial economy, creative industries have been gaining in prominence, and interest in them has been growing since the 1990s. Florida (2002) highlighted the importance of creativity for the future of the economy, arguing that the generation of ideas makes it possible to increase productivity. To attain competitiveness, this author advocates attracting and cultivating what he terms the creative population through autonomy and flexibility, asserting that human creativity is the ultimate economic resource and that the capacity to generate new ideas and better ways to do things is what increases productivity and, therefore, the standard of living. Another author who has focused on creativity's importance for the economic future, drawing special attention to the urban environment, is Landry (2012), who maintains that added value is rather acquired through the use of knowledge applied to products, services, or processes (Landry & Bianchini, 1998). Therefore, creative industries are becoming increasingly important for the economy, not only in terms of employment and production, but also in terms of the technological progress and long-term development of countries (Boix-Domènech & Rausell-Köster, 2018).

The creative industries are defined as "those industries which have their origin in individual creativity, skill and talent and which have a potential for wealth and job creation through the generation and exploitation of intellectual property" (Department for Digital, Culture, Media & Sport, UK Government, 2001). Hartley (2005) defines the creative industries as "the conceptual and practical convergence of the creative arts (individual talent) with cultural industries (mass scale), in the context of the new media technologies (ICTs) within a new knowledge economy, for the use of newly interactive citizen-consumers" (p. 5). Hence, the creative industries can sometimes produce tangible products, but they can also offer intellectual or artistic services, generating creative content (Boix-Domènech & Rausell-Köster, 2018).

DOI: 10.4324/9781003246879-4

Over the years, the academic community has debated which activities should and should not be regarded as creative (Potts, 2011). Initially, activities such as architecture, design, advertising, music, performing arts, etc. were categorized as part of the creative industries. In Cunningham (2002), the list of creative industries includes analogue arts, established commercial business sectors, and digital new economy activities. To Howkins (2001), the creative industries are made up of the copyright, the patent, the trademark, and the design sectors.

Marketing, advertising, and PR are included in the creative industries today. They have their own university studies, companies, and professional associations (Hackley, 2018), although, as we shall see in this chapter, the boundaries between them are sometimes blurred.

4.2 Globalization as a risk and opportunity

With globalization, goods, people, and information can move across borders effortlessly. Globalization has also enabled universal connectivity. However, as CEOs themselves recognize in an international survey conducted by PWC (PwC's 20th CEO survey), it has not contributed to narrowing the gap between rich and poor, nor has it succeeded in making tax systems more equitable, nor has it improved the efforts to combat climate change and the scarcity of natural resources.

PR, marketing, and advertising all contribute to globalization in one way or another, whether through the creation and execution of communication campaigns for international clients, or via the existence within the sector itself of large conglomerates of international communication groups that include agencies from all three branches and operate across several countries. In addition to serving domestic clients, some of these agencies also work with multinational clients. It's important to note that many of these large communication groups are headquartered in Anglo-Saxon countries. Bourne (2016a and 2016b) discusses how globalization has impacted these three professional fields, citing authors such as Witkowski (2008) and Ellis et al. (2011) who have warned of the risk of cultural imperialism that can result from it, which translates into a diffusion of Western values, lifestyles, and attitudes. In this regard, we have already seen in Chapter 1 how authors such as Taylor (2000), *Sriramesh (2010), and Wakefield (2010) highlight the importance of public relations' ability to take into account the sociocultural realities of the country they operate in when developing their communication proposal and also contribute to the social development of that country.*

4.3 Creativity at the core of the advertising practice

Creativity is a concept closely associated with the advertising industry, and there is a large body of literature on creativity in advertising. In fact, creativity has been defined as the most essential element in advertising success (El Murad & West, 2004), and the foundation upon which the advertising business is built and its most valuable resource (Griffin & Morrison, 2010). Bourne (2016a and 2016b) notes that scholars such as McStay (2010) and Nixon (2003) have previously pointed out that advertising has engendered a "cult of creativity" and mythology of "artistry plus genius".

Crawford (2016) points out, however, that "history reveals that advertising's embrace of creativity was constructed rather than innate" (p. 146). This author argues that advertising adopted creativity as its hallmark after the Second World War and the Creative Revolution led by Bill Bernbach in New York in the 1950s and 1960s, when he paired the art director and copywriter in the same team called "the creative duo" (Samuel, 2012). Before that, advertising had to be positioned as a serious business, the result of an in-depth analysis, the application of methodology, and a clear understanding of marketing objectives (Crawford, 2016). With the expansion of advertising agencies after the war, they needed to differentiate themselves from one another. Some agencies were more client-service oriented, while others were more creative. Finally, the industry embraced Koslow et al.'s (2003) definition of advertising creativity as resting on two pillars: originality and appropriateness; that is, as an industry governed by rigorous and methodological criteria that employs creativity to find effective communication solutions for clients.

Furthermore, as we have seen in Chapter 2, the figure of the creative director has played a very important role in advertising for a much longer period of time than it has in PR. Kilgour et al. (2013) state that "the advertising industry is one of the few industries with personnel that specialize in creative idea-generation processes" (p. 164). So, while creative directors exist in almost all advertising agencies, they have yet to become widespread in PR consultancies, although they are gradually making their way there, as evidenced by the fact that if in 2012 only 12% of PR consultancies (The Holmes Report & NowGoCreate, 2013) had a creative director, in 2021 it was 53%, and 12% of them were considering hiring one (PRovoke & Now Go Create, 2021).

Due to the identification of the advertising industry as creative, as well as the convergence brought about by the new digital environment, some clients have opted to hire integrated communication services (including PR solutions) from advertising agencies or, in any case, to hire advertising agencies to generate creative ideas. Recent years, however, have seen a change in this. Respondents to the *2021 Creativity in PR Study* "confirm that their firms have been designated as lead creative agency, which jumps to 59% from 48% when this survey was last conducted in 2017" (PRovoke & Now GoCreate, 2021, p. 21).

4.4 Journalism and PR: from media relations to brand journalism

Journalists have always been key stakeholders in PR. Media relations, the process by which organizations build relationships with journalists, has long been considered as one of the areas of specialization of PR practitioners since the 1920s in the United States, when pioneers such as Ivy Ledbetter Lee (1877–1934), considered the father of modern PR, emerged (Hiebert, 1966). Originally a Wall Street journalist, Lee was hired by the Rockefellers in 1914 to lead highly regarded communication campaigns. He is considered the first professional to incorporate the principles of transparency, accuracy, and truthfulness into the practice of PR, which marked a major departure from how media relations practice developed in the 19th century (Zoch et al., 2014). It was Lee who helped to shift the perception of the PR profession away from the image of journalists' persecutors toward professionals necessary to get truthful and accurate information about organizations they work for (Xifra, 2014). Using accurate data to inform is the guiding principle of media relations and publicity today.

Publicity, understood as earned editorial content obtained from information provided by an organization, for example, in the form of a press release, interview, or a press conference, is a PR practice that is still in use because the media provide credibility when they find that this information is relevant to their audiences. Media relations contribute to an organization's visibility in the eyes of the public and the community (Khodarahmi, 2009). "The media still maintain an important role in validating and approving information from other sources and reinforce influence giving such sources credibility" (Lloyd & Toogood, 2014, p. 108).

However, media consumption habits have changed, the digital transformation has led to the traditional media losing their audience, as well as their monopoly on explaining current affairs. As a result, they have had to reduce staff in some cases and cannot rely on enough specialized professionals. The traditional media are giving way to other forms of content consumption, mostly digital. PR, and specifically media relations, have also been affected by this change, as they have had to evolve and adapt to the proliferation of channels (digital television, cable, digital versions of the press, podcasts, etc.) and to a higher degree of interactivity with users. Online press rooms, social media newsrooms, and specific apps for contacting journalists were among the first initiatives taken by press offices.

Despite the steadily decreasing role of the press office in the PR mix in the recent years (Lalueza & Estanyol, 2021), PR professionals have now to continue collaborating with journalists. It is essential that they know how to adapt content provided that 21st century media are much more interactive, multimedia—with textual, visual, and audio content—and hypertextual (Sánchez-Guijaldo, 2017). They must also adjust to the reality that nowadays anyone can watch whatever content they want anytime and anywhere. Furthermore, segmenting the receivers and de-massifying the communication allows content to be tailored to specific audiences, resulting in much more personalized content.

Traditionally, the relationship between journalists and PR has been based on collaboration but there have also been tensions and a willingness to differentiate between the two disciplines. In fact, PR practitioners working in media relations have been referred to as "the dark side" by journalists. According to Macnamara (2014) "journalists maintain negative perceptions of PR based on narrow understanding of PR" (p. 739).

Even today, some journalists still hold a negative view of PR even though much of the information in the media comes from PR practitioners and many journalists are grateful for their assistance, as they are able to interview newsmakers, obtain data on key sectors, and so on. According to Moloney and McGrath (2019)

> PR and journalism are sufficiently adversarial since journalists critically and objectively evaluate PR communication, which is primarily one-sided advocacy and therefore lacking in objectivity. Such an 'adversarial' relationship is necessary for the retention of the third-party effect provided by the media.
>
> (Auger, 2021, p. 223)

Thus, the activities of media relations require skillful writing, a sense of what makes for good news, as well as knowledge of media work routines (Gregory & Willis, 2013). The fact that this knowledge is often shared by professionals in the media prompted organizations and PR consultancies for years to hire journalists for PR roles—especially in the area of media relations—to the point that journalism degrees were regarded as better equipped than PR degrees. At the same time, many journalism graduates, unable to find work in the media, chose to work in PR.

A practice that falls between journalism and PR is brand journalism, defined by Zerfass et al. (2016) as the production of newsworthy content that takes advantage of journalistic skills to promote a brand. As a result, organizations become news providers by applying journalistic criteria, formats, language, and routines. For example, by publishing customer magazines or websites with articles written by company specialists who are experts in their field. These websites, turned into news portals, are not small publications for niche audiences, but global mega-portals linked to social networks, which compete with traditional media (Barciela, 2013).

Koch et al. (2021) argue that brand journalism "blurs the boundaries between journalism and strategic communication", with its professionals playing a hybrid role between journalists and PR professionals. It can lead to a loss of professional identity (Holton & Molyneux, 2017) or to criticism of the loss of journalistic independence. The reflection on media independence, however, goes beyond these specific works.

4.4.1 Journalism and public relations facing a threat of mistrust and misinformation

Recent years have seen a rise in fake news and disinformation that has only prompted doubts among citizens. Both journalism and PR see this proliferation of disinformation as a threat, which has a lot to do with the new digital channels, where anyone can publish anything and where algorithms favor content with lots of likes over rigorous and contrasted information. In the digital environment, the number of publishers has multiplied exponentially without the mediation of editors, which contributes to even more confusion for users and makes it increasingly difficult to distinguish between genuine and fake content. According to a study by the International Communications Consultancy Organization (ICCO), which represents PR and communications agencies in 70 countries, it is becoming harder and harder to differentiate between accurate information and false news (ICCO, 2020). In turn, according to the *2021 Global Communications Report* (USC Annenberg Center for Public Relations, 2021), 77% of journalists expect the proliferation of fake news and conspiracy theories to increase in the future. The study underlines that "these malicious sources of disinformation are significant contributors to the decay of truth and the polarization of opinion" (p. 27). Recent years have seen a loss of trust in the media among citizens. In fact, more than 60% of citizens have trouble determining whether a news item was created by a reputable media outlet. Edelman's Trust Barometer 2021 attributes this distrust primarily to a significant decline in the credibility of information and communication platforms, especially search engines and social networks.

This is why trust, which has eroded in recent years, because of the COVID-19 pandemic (Edelman's Trust Barometer, 2021) is expected to dominate the profession's agenda in the coming years, according to the European Communication Monitor (EUPRERA, 2021).

Fake news can significantly harm an organization's reputation. It's therefore vital that organizations monitor what's being said about them so that they can respond appropriately. Professionals in PR should work together with journalists to fight fake news, discredit it, and demand ethical communication (Jahng et al., 2020).

Box 4.1

To fight fake news, the United Nations (UN), in collaboration with Purpose, created **Share Verified**, an initiative to combat misinformation about the Coronavirus pandemic. In order to provide accurate information on COVID-19, a website was created (shareverified.com) containing data on the evolution of the pandemic, information about vaccines, advice on avoiding infection, mental health tips, as well as inspirational messages from the greatest human beings. Additionally, the action aimed to involve citizens in the fight against misinformation by providing them with tools to verify information before sharing it on social media. Collaborations were also set up with the social networks themselves to eradicate the hate and vile remarks made about COVID-19 that were proliferating in these media. To this end, the Verified symbol was created to be added to messages shared through social networks that had been verified.

4.4.2 Citizen journalism

Citizens' participation and the creation of content are also common practices in journalism, specifically through citizen journalism. Citizen journalism is defined as being citizen produced, edited, and distributed through self-managed digital platforms, wherein citizens control the entire production process of a news report (Suárez, 2017).

Due to the advancement of the internet and a new digital context, audiences have become more active participants in the media, generating their own content, producing information, and even creating their own media (Sánchez-Guijaldo, 2017). Thanks to new technologies, today, any citizen with a mobile phone and an internet connection can create news pieces, which until recently could only be edited by professionals with specific tools. People around the world can now share texts, audios, and videos on current affairs, becoming producers and disseminators of information. Citizen journalism involves people actively participating in the research, reporting, analyzing, and disseminating of news and information.

Currently, this type of journalism coexists with professional journalism. However, it has its critics as well. Some argue that its results are sometimes of poor quality and, as it is not regulated, can be very subjective. Citizen journalism, according to Suárez (2017), occupies an ambiguous space between the private exercise of communicating and offering testimony, and the social responsibility of the media to inform. Hence, Mutsvairo and Salgado (2022) argue that there should be more discussion on "the conceivability, capacity, reliability, and acceptability of citizen journalists" (p. 354).

Box 4.2

The war in Ukraine, which began in February 2022, could be followed in real time. Numerous citizens' testimonies were broadcast by the media right from the beginning. At the same time, numerous citizens gave first-person accounts of fleeing their homes and the trauma of becoming refugees through stories, information, photos, and videos posted to social media like Instagram, Twitter, Tik Tok, Facebook, and YouTube.

4.5 PR and graphic design

It is important for organizations to have a visual identity. Especially nowadays, when visual communication is increasingly important, as we see in social media. Therefore, graphic design is crucial for corporate communication, since it influences the way the audience perceives organizations. In fact, graphic design has always been considered a creative industry.

The logo, product packaging, facility design, website design, etc. are all elements that communicate and must be aligned with the mission, vision, and values of an organization. Using typography, colors, and shapes, graphic design becomes a tool for communicating the identity of an organization both internally and externally.

It is therefore necessary for the communication professionals of an organization to have a corporate visual identity manual that includes guidelines about the application of the logo, typography, colors, as well as how the materials should appear in the different formats and elements (business cards, letters, brochures, web, social networks, posters, merchandise, spaces, etc.). Nowadays, many corporate visual identity manuals also include image banks, sound marks, and audiovisual masks. These manuals are very useful for designing graphic pieces since they provide the designers with the same guidelines so they can create them under the same visual and graphic paradigm.

Furthermore, our society has become increasingly visual. As social networks and smartphones have become more prevalent, video and image content has skyrocketed. Instagram, for instance, places a great deal of emphasis on images, while on Tik Tok and YouTube it is videos that play a key role, so editing the visual content in a way that is attractive will also be critically important. Additionally, it is known that online content in visual format results in better engagement, message retention, and virality. Tamble (2019) reports that "content with relevant images gets 94% more views than content without relevant images; and infographics grow 12% more traffic, and 200% more shares than posts without images". As a matter of fact, the brain is better at remembering images than it is at remembering written text. In addition, images are a universal language. Therefore, when planning a PR campaign through social networks, a good graphic design will be very helpful when sharing content. For instance, using infographics, illustrations, or photo and text designs. Content such as images with phrases is shared more often on social networks because it establishes a link between the visual and the emotional.

Communication and PR professionals usually prepare the briefings for graphic designers to develop the visual identity and corporate graphics manual. Graphic designers sometimes work at the same in-house communication department. In other cases, agencies offer overlapped services. Schultz and Ervolder (1998) examined how PR consultancies, advertising agencies and design studios offer services that often overlap, resulting in takeovers and alliances, and in the emergence of new agencies offering integrated communication solutions such as corporate image building, product image building, and visual corporate identity.

Traditionally, as we saw in Chapter 1, it is PR professionals who develop the corporate identity of an organization, helping to define its mission, vision, and values, as well as to establish lines of communication with different stakeholders, while the corporate visual identity is created by graphic designers. It is important, however, for both professionals to work together. As Sgarbossa (n.d.) observes

> it will be interesting to discuss whether the designer should be trained in strategy, or whether PR practitioners should learn about graphic design, or whether both professionals should do so in order to take a quality step and begin working in an interdisciplinary manner.

4.6 The art of persuasion

Although marketing, advertising, and PR sometimes serve an informative purpose, most of the time they are used to persuade key audiences, understanding persuasion as the capacity to influence people by offering reasons and arguments to think, feel, or act in a certain way. A persuasive communication aims to change the receiver's outlook, behavior, attitude, or perception. However, persuasion should not be confused with manipulation, which attempts to influence others by hiding the truth or distorting of reality.

The nature of advertising has been considered persuasive communication from its inception, however, as Miles (2013) points out, the concept has generated more controversy in some of the PR and marketing literature.

Moloney and McGrath (2019) argue that PR should reclaim the principles of persuasion and influence as the bedrock of its practice, as this better reflects the reality of an industry that aims to influence public behavior and public opinion (Auger, 2021). Pfau and Wan (2006) support this view, arguing that persuasion remains a fundamental element of modern PR practice. PR scholars such as Miller (2017) have explored the relationship between effective persuasion and effective PR, while Fawkes (2007) has examined its ethical implications.

4.7 Integrated Marketing Communication (IMC)

Marketing, advertising, and PR were brought together in the late 1980s as part of the IMC, which culminated in the founding of the School of Integrated Communication. This, in turn, consisted of two strands: Total Communication and Corporate Communication. Integrated Communication was defined as combining all communication efforts of an organization, including advertising, direct marketing, promotions, and PR, in order to maximize the effects of communication and achieve the organization's goals (Anantachart, 2006). It is the process by which a company integrates and coordinates its communication channels to create a clear, coherent, and compelling message about the company and its products (Kotler et al., 2000). Xifra (2014) defines IMC as a strategy in which PR lends its techniques to a marketing strategy for a product or service. Rose (1996) notes that IMC was advocated by such scholars as Caywood et al. (1991), Schultz, Tannenbaum & Lauterborn (1993), Newsom et al. (1992), Duncan et al. (1993), and Harris (1998), but also disapproved by theorists such as Dozier and Lauzen (1990) and Grunig (2009) who viewed it as an intrusion of marketing into PR. This point was also made by Kitchen et al. (2004) and Christensen et al. (2005). Smith (2013) believes that coordinating marketing and PR can help improve the achievement of organizational goals. Accordingly, "from the perspective of integrated marketing communication, advertising can be seen as a tool for both public relations and marketing" (Smith, 2013, p. 12)

In the early 2000s, Hutton (2001) encouraged the field of PR to attempt to differentiate itself from other disciplines such as marketing and advertising but warned theorists that pursing differentiation would result in the discipline remaining disconnected from the constant evolution that marketing is also undergoing at both the theoretical and professional levels.

In fact, marketing is becoming increasingly aware of the need to build long-term relationships with a wide variety of audiences, moving away from the hard sell approach (Pavlou & Stewart, 2000; Du Plessis, 2010), as well as promoting a more dialogical and conversational approach with consumers (Seran & Izvercian, 2014). Marketing communication is increasingly

taking into account collaborative dialogue, that is, it is committed to building bridges of dialogue and collaboration with audiences, who are increasingly being studied more individually (Kent & Taylor, 2002; Daymon &
Holloway, 2010). In addition, mass communication aimed at persuading
audiences is more costly if the audience is very specific. Personalized and
targeted communication is therefore much more effective. As Smith (2013)
notes, "the key is to respect the complementary roles of marketing and public relations while maximizing the potential of cooperation and coordina-
tion" (p. 9).

4.8 Boundaries between disciplines blurring in the digital environment

New technologies and the digital environment have changed and will continue to change the way companies, public sector entities, brands, countries,
and individuals communicate with their audiences. Persuasive communication is undergoing a profound transformation, with implications for marketing, traditional approaches to advertising creating great opportunities
for PR.

New technologies have given way to the possibility of personalizing
mass communication much more and directing it to more specific audiences. New communication channels have contributed to changing the way
audiences are viewed by organizations, moving from passive, anonymous
audiences to participants who act as both senders and co-creators of communication content.

Daymon and Holloway (2010) suggest that it is no longer sufficient
for organizations to communicate a desired identity or project the potential benefits of a brand or an organization if they have not first listened to,
appreciated, and considered the concerns and opinions of the audiences they
are trying to reach. The digital environment demands that marketers, advertisers, and PR professionals place even greater emphasis on active listening
to what their audiences are interested in, as well as on establishing conversations and, consequently, more two-way communication that transcends
the largely one-way communication of previous eras.

As a results, organizations are looking for less intrusive communication
and more voluntary consuming formats that, instead of constantly contacting their audiences, offer quality content and help to the people who are
truly interested in them. Today it is no longer enough to tell how good an
organization is at doing things; rather, it is for audiences to value it for
helping them make better choices by providing better information about
issues they care about, on which the organization has something relevant
to contribute.

The technological transformation has enabled many processes to be automated. The PR industry is adapting to the digital environment, integrating specialized professionals, creating new divisions, and offering new services. However, there is competition in some of these new services not only within the sector itself, but also in the contiguous industries such as marketing, advertising, journalism, and graphic design. The cross-disciplinary creative teams working in these industries have adapted the communication strategy and the message through the application of a variety of techniques and channels to target-specific audiences, sometimes making it difficult to distinguish one form of communication from another. At the industry level, Schultz and Ervolder (1998) noted that design studios are integrating communication units, advertising agencies are offering PR services, and PR agencies are developing corporate identity frameworks.

Integration of PR, marketing, and advertising techniques will become increasingly common. Instead of being viewed as a threat and creating walls of containment, it should help the PR industry to open up to new manifestations and all available communication channels in order to engage audiences, without compromising its core: establishing relationships of trust between organizations and stakeholders.

4.9 Convergence of marketing, advertising, and PR

Digitalization has blurred the lines between marketing, advertising, and PR more than ever before. The convergence of these trends has been explored by authors such as Richards and Curran (2002), Hallahan (2007), Hallahan et al. (2007), Hutton (2001), Estanyol (2012), McKie and Willis (2012), Bourne (2016a, 2016b), and Hackley (2018), among others. According to Bourne (2016a), "in an increasingly globalized and digital world, distinctions between advertising, marketing and PR are often blurred and perceived as part of the same set of advanced techniques in modern commercial culture" (p. 30). Even more pronounced is this convergence in online consumer marketing campaigns (Estanyol, 2012).

Advertising has traditionally been oriented toward more commercial objectives like promotion of products or services, brand repositioning, or customer loyalty, while PR have worked on building relationships with all stakeholders, consumers being just one of them, and seeking to achieve favorable opinions and always protect the reputation of an organization. Hybrid formats, however, are emerging today that challenge the traditional classification of disciplines.

According to the channels used, PR largely focused on earned media and owned media, while marketing and advertising largely utilized paid media. Today, however, many journalistic approaches are applied in owned media, journalists are often involved in the preparation of content, and, as we have already discussed, brand journalism is a technique that balances journalism with PR.

Moreover, it is in the field of shared media that the boundaries are blurring even more, with more shared initiatives that use hybrid techniques based on content creation. Techniques that are given new terms that become synonyms depending on whether they are used by digital marketing, advertising, or PR (Macnamara, 2014).

According to Estanyol and Willis (2019), who analyzed the most successful PR campaigns in 2018, there has been a shift in emphasis in PR away from mass media (although it is still very important) toward owned and shared media (websites, blogs, podcasts, and apps), and today PR agencies are seeking to position themselves as experts in branded content. The increasing requirement from organizations and brands for online content which can be shared across multiple media channels creates a landscape where the roles and responsibilities are attributed to different communication disciplines is both contested and controversial (Ihlen & Pallas, 2014; Helgason, 2016; Macnamara et al., 2016).

4.10 Content creation using hybrid techniques

Content creation is a practice shared by journalism, marketing, PR, advertising, and other industries. Professionals who are able to develop new original content that stands out and attracts audiences are in demand. For this purpose, Bourne (2016a) reminds us, marketing, advertising, and PR need professionals with excellent communication skills. These include mastering digital narratives (Aced, 2020).

Content generation leads to "convergence of the cultures of media production and consumption" (Deuze, 2007, p. 244), and the emergence of the concept of *prosumer*, which Alvin Toffler formulated in 1980 as a synthesis of producer and consumer. When it comes to persuasive communication, it implies that consumers not only care about receiving information about products and services but are also active in sharing their opinions and experiences about them.

With the explosion of social media, the power of *prosumers* has increased exponentially as the content they now produce, for example in the form of positive or negative reviews of certain companies, products, and brands, can have a significant impact on their reputation. In fact, according to Kaemingk (2020), 93% of customers read online reviews before purchasing a product, which highlights the importance of making these reviews as positive as possible. As Peláez, 2020 reminds us, the online opinions of other consumers create more trust among consumers who are in the buying decision-making process, which is why online word-of-mouth has become such a critical element. This new scenario calls on organizations to develop strategies that involve *prosumers* and make them brand ambassadors (Seran & Izvercian, 2014). To accomplish this, it is necessary to incorporate creativity into the development of new content that can be shared online.

Box 4.3

Among the platforms consumers most often use when rating products, restaurants, hotels, or other services are Amazon, TripAdvisor, or Yelp.

In the online environment, prosumers' opinions and ratings are not only shared between them and brands or companies, but also between themselves, resulting in a great deal of communication that circulates through digital channels. As Moloney and McGrath (2019) and Auger (2021) point out, positive comments posted online by audiences about a company can positively influence its reputation; however, negative reviews also have effects, adverse ones in this case, which may compromise a company's reputation and credibility. Comments, whether positive or negative, can come from customers, but also from other audiences, such as employees, suppliers, etc. Therefore, it is crucial for organizations to identify these contents and their authors, as well as to establish and maintain good relations with these new *prosumers*, starting with active listening, as this is crucial for improving their products, services, or their own behavior in society.

Another phenomenon to be aware of is malicious or fake reviews, which go beyond sincere criticism from a user, as they can result from a variety of sources, from bots making fake reviews to orchestrated campaigns run by competitors or groups opposed to the organization. These fake reviews can also severely damage the reputation of a brand or organization. In this case, it is important to identify them, contact the platforms, report them, and activate the crisis communication plan.

4.10.1 User-generated content

User-generated content (UGC) is defined as a content that is produced voluntarily by individuals and has the potential to generate conversations in the digital environment, as well as create engagement (Borst, 2019). Marketers, advertising agencies, and PR have been observing UGC with great interest ever since its inception, implementing strategies to include it in their communication campaigns. For example, earned content can be the result of a PR campaign (the organization making a public comment on social networks), or it can be the result of the organization encouraging users to share its content through contests and sweepstakes, which would be more like a marketing strategy.

By using UGC, organizations are able to involve more people in the creation of their communication, the users themselves. Users can share texts, photographs, and videos that reflect their own style, which can connect them with other users with similar tastes and interests.

Box 4.4

GoPro is one of the companies that use UGC to promote their brand. Aside from creating professional content, the company encourages its community to share private videos they record with their sports cameras, resulting in high-quality content in very diverse environments around the world. Many of these videos are then shared on GoPro's social media channels, including YouTube, Facebook, Vimeo, and Instagram. GoPro organizes contests and engages celebrities to share content, in this case paid content.

As Hackley (2018) points out, paid content can be created and then uploaded to YouTube and/or the brand's website as part of the advertising, but when this content goes viral, PR techniques are applied.

4.10.2 Developing influencer relationships

With influencer relations, it can also be difficult to determine whether the technique is marketing, advertising, or PR. Unpaid collaborations are typically conducted under the umbrella of PR, whereas when there is a financial incentive involved, they are more likely to be marketing or advertising agreements. In Chapter 3, we saw how important it is to establish and maintain good relationships with influencers, especially when they share similar values and post about brands, thereby giving them more credibility and notoriety. Janssen et al. (2022) point out that "the persuasive power of influencers seems to originate from their unique positioning as authentic, relatable, and accessible 'superpeers'" (p. 104).

It is a growing trend to use influencer marketing in social media communication. Influencer marketing involves establishing collaborative links—generally paid—between brands, organizations, and influencers so that they share content in their social networks regarding the brand or organization's products or services (Campbell & Farrell, 2020). Influencers thus become brand endorsers.

It is a growing industry that has seen an increase in the number of agencies providing services to manage influencer relationships. According to "The State of Influencer Marketing 2021: Benchmark Report" by Influencer Marketing Hub, 62% of marketers say they intend to increase their influencer marketing budget in the next few years. Furthermore, many agencies and companies are planning to allocate a higher share of their budgets to influencer marketing, which could reach close to 40% of total marketing spending. According to Santora (2022), the growth of influencer marketing is largely attributed

to the increasing popularity of short video formats on platforms like TikTok, Facebook, and YouTube, the effect of the global pandemic on consumers, which catalyzed social media consumption, and the optimization of data collection, which marketers used for social media ads.

Campbell and Farrell (2020) note that the recent growth of influencer marketing is also attributable to shifts in media consumption from print to online media as well as the emergence of social networks as forums for consumers to share their opinions about products and services.

In the beginning, companies such as those in the fashion, beauty, and lifestyle sectors hired bloggers to promote their products and services, however today, the range of companies using this marketing strategy has grown, and instagrammers and youtubers are among the most sought-after profiles. TikTok has also become a very attractive platform for marketing departments. As Statista (2021) states, "what makes TikTok marketing so appealing are the app's striking download figures, audience reach, and the impressive engagement rates of influencer content – especially among Gen Z users".

Influencers have become, as we saw in Chapter 3, a key element in PR, marketing, and advertising campaigns.

4.10.3 Interactive advertising

Traditionally, advertising used unidirectional messages, whereas PR included bidirectionality as part of its ideal. Our understanding of this is postulated, as we saw in Chapter 1, by the model of excellence in PR proposed by Grunig (1992) and by the dialogic theory of Kent and Taylor (2002). However, in the new digital environment, advertising is looking for new methods that are less intrusive, such as interactive advertising, which enables the user to make decisions and have control over the way the message is received. The user can select from several options, request more information, etc. As Pavlou and Stewart (2000) and Leckenby and Li (2000) highlight, interactive advertising reduces information asymmetry and promotes trust through information exchange. Even so, it cannot be forgotten that the main objective is to encourage and/or influence consumers' purchasing decisions.

Interactive advertising may utilize traditional media (billboards, etc.) or be developed on the Internet, social networks, or applications. As a matter of fact, interactive advertising is primarily used on smartphones, tablets, smart TVs, computers, and other technological devices.

Interactive advertising is a booming industry, as evidenced by the data provided by the Interactive Advertising Bureau (IAB), the association that brings together interactive advertising companies in the world's main markets.

4.10.4 Native advertising, sponsored content, digital storytelling, advertiser-funded media content, and transmedia branding

Another example of convergence is *native advertising*, which is online advertising that closely resembles the style and format of the platform it is featured on and, according to Hackley (2018), is a hybrid genre that combines PR and sponsorship, and can be confused with editorial content, which has ethical implications since it can confuse the recipient about the independence of journalism and undermine its credibility.

In Chapter 3, we discussed *digital storytelling*, another practice that has spread among advertising, content marketing, and PR, and it is often difficult to draw a line between them.

Digital storytelling is used, for example, in advertiser funded media content, films which have their own narrative, produced by brands that are shared and viewed on social networks. The challenge is to create content that users really want to see. The technique goes beyond product placement because the product does not appear in a film or series on a one-time, passive basis, but rather, the brand creates an ongoing narrative that is related to the product or service it wants to promote. Moreover, the story often revolves around the brand's values, not on its products or services, and is intended to generate conversation and notoriety around it, as well as achieve a high level of virality.

In addition to digital storytelling, *transmedia branding* is another advertising technique. A lot of its content relies on fiction and is meant to be less intrusive than traditional advertising. Tenderich and Williams (2014) defines it as "a communication process in which information about a brand is packaged into an integrated story, which is dispersed in unique contributions across multiple media channels for the purpose of creating an interactive and engaging brand experience" (p. 16). Hence, transmedia branding employs transmedia storytelling to create an appealing and participatory brand experience for the audience, thereby generating prosumer engagement (Du Plessis, 2019). From the perspective of strategic communication, it is important that the brand's values are reflected in the stories it tells.

4.10.5 Sponsored content, branded content, and content marketing

An approach that is very similar to this is *branded content*, which we discussed in our previous chapter and which, beyond video, can be found in various formats, including podcasts, interactive pieces, video games, etc. This is brand-created content that is intended to entertain, and which can, in turn, be co-created with users, who can tell their stories and experiences with the brand or organization.

In the same way, *content marketing* is defined as "a strategic marketing approach focused on creating and distributing valuable, relevant, and consistent content to attract and retain a clearly defined audience – and, ultimately, to drive profitable customer action" (Content Marketing Institute, n.d.). Patrutiu (2015) asserts that content marketing has become an essential tool of digital campaigns. Content marketing can take the form of newsletters, podcasts, infographics, FAQs, eBooks, questionnaires, etc. Similarly, it can also be an article, an image, or a data sheet, generally designed to drive traffic to a website. Companies use content marketing to help their target audiences resolve their doubts and become authorities on particular topics.

Sponsored content, similar to *brand journalism*, is a hybrid technique that combines advertising, PR, and journalism. While branded content is created exclusively by the brand, sponsored content is created in collaboration between the editorial team of a media outlet and the brand. It is not publicity because it is not produced by earned media, however, it would be more like an advertorial, which is the result of fusing the words advertising and editorial, i.e., more akin to the advertorials that used to appear in print media.

4.11 Implications from an ethical perspective

Marketing, advertising, journalism, and PR have all been able to benefit from the emergence of these hybrid techniques. Due to the crisis of traditional advertising and the decline of traditional media audiences, these industries have adopted new formats in the digital environment. Formats that blur the line between branded content and editorial content. Moreover, this type of content is sometimes created by journalists, sometimes by advertisers, and sometimes by PR professionals. These services are provided by these industries to finance themselves (in the case of the media) as well as to provide a more comprehensive service to their clients (in the case of marketing, advertising, and PR agencies). There is a need for discipline reflection because sometimes techniques are adopted that aren't aligned with the traditional definition of the discipline. Also necessary are ethical reflections, because audiences receiving this content are often unable to discern what has been paid for by a brand or an organization from free information provided by a media outlet or influencer. The receiver is faced with very ambiguous formats. It is also important to consider how to preserve the credibility of this content. Content that, despite being paid for, should provide value and be rigorous and truthful. Nevertheless, as we mentioned in Chapter 1, it is necessary to always follow professional ethics and, in cases of doubt, to consult the codes of ethics existing in the different disciplines, which must also be tailored to this new hybrid context.

4.12 Creativity awards

In the advertising industry, where creativity is a distinguishing feature, as we have seen, creative festivals are strongly promoted and some of them have become international benchmarks, such as the Clio Awards. Besides serving as professional recognition, these competitions contribute to the legitimacy and social promotion of the advertising profession, as well as serving as a promotional tool for advertising agencies to build up loyalty, attract new clients, and recruit talent. According to Kilgour et al. (2013), creativity awards have become an important consideration for certain clients when it comes to selecting an advertising agency, since they consider them an indicator of success. A prize in these competitions can also be a source of internal motivation and an inspiration for agencies. However, Kilgour et al. (2013) warn against what they call the existence of an *original bias*, in the sense that "most award-winning work is rarely regarded as being highly strategic" (p. 163). In other words, strategy and appropriateness, other aspects of creativity, "are not adequately, nor proportionately, considered" (p. 168).

However, participation in creativity festivals has historically been low in the PR industry, although there are also PR awards recognizing creativity, either because it is an element that is specially valued by the members of the jury or because they have dedicated categories for creativity, such as the IPRA Gold World Awards for Excellence in Public Relations.

Moreover, there are festivals devoted to creativity, such as the Cannes Creativity Awards, with categories for different communication specialties, where both advertising and PR campaigns may be submitted. However, even today these festivals have a longer tradition among the advertising sector, and their prize winners continue to be dominated by advertising agencies, even in the PR categories. "Yet advertising's supposed dominance over creativity may have infringed on PR territory in some contexts" (Bourne, 2016a, p. 37).

In fact, after the Cannes PR Lions 2021, it was once again confirmed that creative leadership remains dominated by ad agencies (Sudhaman, 2021a).

Aslan and Ertem-Eray (2018) analyzed the most awarded campaigns at the 2015, 2016 and 2017 PR Week Awards, concluding that "being original but still adaptive, new and quite functional can be key to having successful creative campaigns" (p. 193).

A recent study by Estanyol and Willis (2019) examined 275 award-winning campaigns and agencies of four international contests [Cannes Lions PR, Global EFFIE Awards, IPRA's Golden Awards for Excellence in Public Relations, and Global SABRE (Superior Achievement in Branding and Reputation Awards)] held during 2018. The trends identified among the most awarded campaigns include the use of (1) video content (and branded content, specifically online); (2) owned media and shared media; (3) storytelling and narrative; (4) gamification; (5) emotion and humor; (6) novelty, surprise, and unexpected elements to motivate and engage; (7) and recognition of responsibility, values, and purpose. In 2021, "when asked what drives great PR work, agency respondents selected authenticity ahead of engagement, courage and storytelling" (Sudhaman, 2021b). Additionally, one of the trends observed in these competitions is the integration of advertising, marketing, and PR.

4.13 Adapting to a changing context

Throughout the decades, PR has evolved to adapt to changes in the social, economic, cultural, and technological environment. As we have seen, the new digital communicative context and social networks in recent years have facilitated the adoption by organizations of new communicative approaches and languages that make full use of all the potentialities at a format level, far beyond traditional text to audiovisual language (infographics, photographs, videos, podcasts, gifs, and so on) and communication style (more informative or entertaining). A digital narrative that requires new approaches to creative models and content development.

Many of these techniques take advantage of the possibility of more direct communication with audiences through interactive formats, encouraging feedback through comments, or even including users as co-creators of content. Professionals in PR have never had so many channels and tools at their disposal to engage with a company's stakeholders. However, it remains to be seen how new communication techniques can be adapted to make them more personalized and appealing to key audiences.

References

Aced, C. (2020). *Nuevas narrativas digitales. Herramientas de storytelling digital para relaciones públicas, periodismo y marca personal.* Amazon Kindle.

Anantachart, S. (2006). Integrated marketing communications and market planning: Their implications to brand equity building. *Journal of Promotion Management, 11*(1), 101–125. https://doi.org/10.1300/J057v11n01_07

Aslan, P., & Ertem-Eray, T. (2018). Creativity in public relations: What do award-winning campaigns tell us? In S. Bowman, et al. (Ed.), *Public relations and the power of creativity.* Emerald Publishing Limited.

Auger, G. (2021). Rethinking public relations: Persuasion, democracy, and society (3rd edition). *Public Relations Education, 7*(1), 220–226.

Barciela, F. (2013). El último desafío, el 'brand journalism'. *Cuadernos de periodistas, 26*, 125–136. www.cuadernosdeperiodistas.com/media/2013/12/Barciela1.pdf

Boix-Domènech, R., & Rausell-Köster, P. (2018). The economic impact of the creative industry in the European Union. In V. Santamarina-Campos & M. Segarra-Oña (Eds.), *Drones and the creative industry* (pp. 19–36). Springer.

Borst, S. (2019, May 15). The rise of UGC in marketing and advertising (and why it's distinctly different from influencer marketing). *International Advertising Bureau (IAB).* www.iab.com/blog/2019ugcbuyersguide/

Bourne, C. D. (2016a). Extending PR's critical conversations with advertising and marketing. *Comunicacao, Midia E Consumo, 13*(38), 29–47. http://dx.doi.org/10.18568/cmc.v13i38.1235

Bourne, C. D. (2016b). Extending PR's critical conversations with advertising and marketing. In J. L'Etang, D. McKie, N. Snow, & J. Xifra (Eds.), *The Routledge handbook of critical public relations* (pp. 119–129). Routledge.

Campbell, C., & Farrell, J. R. (2020). More than meets the eye: The functional components underlying influencer marketing. *Business Horizons, 63*(4), 469–479. https://doi.org/10.1016/j.bushor.2020.03.003

Caywood, C. L., Schultz, D., & Wang, P. (1991). Integrated marketing communications: A survey of national consumer goods advertisers: Research and Report. Northwestern University.

Christensen, L. T., Torp, S., & Firat, A. F. (2005). Integrated marketing communication and postmodernity: An odd couple? *Corporate Communications: An International Journal, 10*(2), 156–167.

Content Marketing Institute. (n.d.). *What is content marketing?* https://contentmarketinginstitute.com/what-is-content-marketing/

Crawford, R. (2016). Creating a creative industry: Australian advertising agencies in the 1960s – 1970s. *Creative Industries Journal, 9*(2), 146–161.

Cunningham, S. (2002). From cultural to creative industries: Theory, industry, and policy implications. *Media International Australia, 102*(1), 54–65. https://doi.org/10.1177/1329878X0210200107

Daymon, C., & Holloway, I. (2010). *Qualitative research methods in public relations and marketing communications*. Routledge.

Department for Digital, Culture, Media & Sport, UK Government. (2001). *Creative industries mapping documents 2001*. www.gov.uk/government/publications/creative-industries-mapping-documents-2001

Deuze, M. (2007). Convergence culture in the creative industries. *International Journal of Cultural Studies, 10*(2), 243–263. https://doi.org/10.1177/1367877907076793

Dozier, D. M., & Lauzen, M. M. (1990). Antecedents and consequences of marketing imperialism on the public relations function. Paper presented at the Annual Convention of the Association for Education in Journalism, Minneapolis, MN.

Duncan, T., Caywood, C., & Newsom, D. (1993). *Preparing advertising and public relations students for the communications industry in the 21st century*. AEJMC Task Force on Integrated Communications.

Du Plessis, C. (2019). Prosumer engagement through story-making in transmedia branding. *International Journal of Cultural Studies, 22*(1), 175–192. https://doi.org/10.1177/1367877917750445

Du Plessis, T. C. (2010). Theoretical guidelines for social media marketing communication. *Communicare: Journal for Communication Sciences in Southern Africa, 29*(1), 1–20.

Edelman. (2021). Edelman's Trust Barometer 2021. https://www.edelman.com/trust/2021-trust-barometer

Ellis, N., Fitchett, J., Higgins, M., Jack, G., Lim, M., Saren, M., & Tadajewski, M. (2011). *Marketing: A critical textbook*. SAGE.

El-Murad, J., & West, D. C. (2004). The definition and measurement of creativity: what do we know? *Journal of Advertising Research, 44*(2), 188–201.

Estanyol, E. (2012). Marketing, public relations, and how Web 2.0 is changing their relationship: A qualitative assessment of PR consultancies operating in Spain. *Public Relations Review, 38*(5), 831–837. https://doi.org/10.1016/j.pubrev.2012.04.006

Estanyol, E., & Willis, P. (2019, July 1 and 2). "PREXIT? An analysis of international award-winning public relations campaigns". Barcelona PR Meeting 2019. Critical intersections: Communication, Public Relations and beyond in a time of convergence.

European Public Relations Education and Research Association (EUPRERA) (2021). *European Communication Monitor 2021*. https://www.communicationmonitor.eu/2021/05/21/ecm-european-communication-monitor-2021/

Fawkes, J. (2007). Public relations models and persuasion ethics: A new approach. *Journal of Communication Management, 11*(4), 313–331. https://doi.org/10.1108/13632540710843922

Florida, R. (2002). *The rise of the creative class* (Vol. 9). Basic Books.

Gregory, A., & Willis, P. (2013). *Strategic public relations leadership*. Routledge.

Griffin, W. G., & Morrison, D. (2010). *The creative process illustrated: How advertising's big ideas are born*. Simon and Schuster.

Grunig, J. E. (1992). *Excellence in public relations and communication management*. Lawrence Erlbaum Associates, Hillsdale, NJ.

Grunig, J. E. (2009). Paradigms of global public relations in an age of digitalisation. *PRism, 6*(2), 1–19.

Hackley, C. (2018). Advertising, marketing and PR: Deepening mutuality amidst a convergent media landscape. In J. Hardy, H. Powell, & I. MacRury (Eds.), *The advertising handbook* (pp. 58–68). Routledge.

Hallahan, K. (2007). Integrated communication: Implications for public relations beyond excellence. *The future of excellence in public relations and communication management*, 299–336.

Hallahan, K., Holtzhausen, D., Van Ruler, B., Verčič, D., & Sriramesh, K. (2007). Defining strategic communication. *International Journal of Strategic Communication, 1*(1), 3–35.

Harris, T. L. (1998). *Value-added public relations: The secret weapon of integrated marketing*. NTC Business Books.

Hartley, J. (2005). *Creative industries*. Blackwell.

Helgason, G. (2016). *Creativity in PR: Exploring the value of creativity in public relations and PR industry awards* (Dissertation). University of Westminster.

Hiebert, R. E. (1966). Ivy Lee: "Father of modern public relations". *The Princeton University Library Chronicle, 27*(2), 113–120.

Holton, A. E., & Molyneux, L. (2017). Identity lost? The personal impact of brand journalism. *Journalism, 18*(2), 195–210. https://doi.org/10.1177/1464884915608816

Howkins, J. (2001). *The creative economy: How people make money from ideas*. The Penguin Press.

Hutton, J. G. (2001). Defining the relationship between public relations and marketing. Public relations' most important challenge. In R. L. Heath (Ed.), *The Sage handbook of public relations* (pp. 509–522). SAGE.

Ihlen, Ø., & Pallas, J. (2014). Mediatization of corporations. In K. Lundby (Ed.), *Handbook on mediatization of communication* (pp. 423–441). De Gruyter Mouton.

Influencer Marketing Hub. (2021). The state of influencer marketing 2021: Benchmark report. *Influencer Marketing Hub*. https://influencermarketinghub.com/influencer-marketing-benchmark-report-2021/

International Communications Consultancy Organization (ICCO). (2020). *ICCO World PR Report 2020*. https://iccopr.com/wp-content/uploads/2021/03/ICCO-report-2020-AMENDS-MARCH-2021.pdf

Interactive Advertising Bureau (IAB). www.iab.com

Jahng, M. R., Lee, H., & Rochadiat, A. (2020). Public relations practitioners' management of fake news: Exploring key elements and acts of information authentication. *Public Relations Review, 46*(2), 101907. https://doi.org/10.1016/j.pubrev.2020.101907

Janssen, L., Schouten, A. P., & Croes, E. A. (2022). Influencer advertising on Instagram: product-influencer fit and number of followers affect advertising outcomes and influencer evaluations via credibility and identification. *International Journal of Advertising, 41*(1), 101–127. https://doi.org/10.1080/02650487.2021.1994205

Kaemingk, D. (2020, October 30). Online reviews statistics to know in 2022. *Qualtrics*. www.qualtrics.com/blog/online-review-stats/

Kent, M. L., & Taylor, M. (2002). Toward a dialogic theory of public relations. Public Relations Review, 28(1), 21–37.

Khodarahmi, E. (2009). Media relations. *Disaster Prevention and Management, 18*(5), 535–540. https://doi.org/10.1108/09653560911003732

Kilgour, M., Sasser, S., & Koslow, S. (2013). Creativity awards: Great expectations? *Creativity Research Journal, 25*(2), 163–171. https://doi.org/10.1080/10400419.2013.783741

Kitchen, P. J., Brignell, J., Li, T., & Jones, G. S. (2004). The emergence of IMC: A theoretical perspective. *Journal of Advertising Research, 44*(1), 19–30.

Koch, T., Viererbl, B., & Schulz-Knappe, C. (2021). How much journalism is in brand journalism? How brand journalists perceive their roles and blur the boundaries between journalism and strategic communication. *Journalism*. https://doi.org/10.1177/14648849211029802

Koslow, S., Sasser, S. L., & Riordan, E. A. (2003). What is creative to whom and why? Perceptions in advertising agencies. *Journal of advertising Research, 43*(1), 96–110. https://doi.org/10.1017/S0021849903030113

Kotler, P., Armstrong, G., Saunders, J., Wong, V., Miquel, S., Bigné, E., & Cámara, D. (2000). *Introducción al marketing*. Pearson Prentice Hall.

Lalueza, F., & Estanyol, E. (2021). La insoportable levedad de los medios. Factores que inciden en la caída del peso de la función de gabinete de prensa en el mix de las relaciones públicas. XV Congreso Internacional de Investigación en Relaciones Públicas, Asociación de Investigadores en Relaciones Públicas (AIRP), 2021, June 30, July 1 and 2. Pontevedra. Spain.

Landry, C. (2012). *The creative city: A toolkit for urban innovators*. Routledge.

Landry, C., & Bianchini, F. (1998). *The creative city*. Demos.

Leckenby, J. D., & Li, H. (2000). From the editors: Why we need the Journal of Interactive Advertising. *Journal of Interactive Advertising, 1*(1), 1–3. https://doi.org/10.1080/15252019.2000.10722039

Lloyd, J., & Toogood, L. (2014). *Journalism and PR: News media and public relations in the digital age*. Bloomsbury Publishing.

Macnamara, J. (2014). Journalism – PR relations revisited: The good news, the bad news, and insights into tomorrow's news. *Public Relations Review, 40*(5), 739–750. https://doi.org/10.1016/j.pubrev.2014.07.002

Macnamara, J., Lwin, M., Adi, A., & Zerfass, A. (2016). 'PESO' media strategy shifts to 'SOEP': Opportunities and ethical dilemmas. *Public Relations Review, 42*(3), 377–385. https://doi.org/10.1016/j.pubrev.2016.03.001

McKie, D., & Willis, P. (2012). Renegotiating the terms of engagement: Public relations, marketing, and contemporary challenges. *Public Relations Review, 38*(5), 846–852. https://doi.org/10.1016/j.pubrev.2012.03.008

McStay, A. (2010). *Digital advertising*. Palgrave Macmillan.

Miles, C. (2013). Persuasion, marketing communication, and the metaphor of magic. *European Journal of Marketing, 47*(11/12), 2002–2019. https://doi.org/10.1108/EJM-11-2011-0632

Miller, G. R. (2017). Persuasion and public relations: Two "Ps" in a pod. In C. H. Botan & V. Hazleton (Eds.), *Public relations theory* (pp. 45–66). Routledge.

Moloney, K., & McGrath, C. (2019). *Rethinking public relations: Persuasion, democracy and society*. Routledge.

Mutsvairo, B., & Salgado, S. (2022). Is citizen journalism dead? An examination of recent developments in the field. *Journalism, 23*(2), 354–371. https://doi.org/10.1177/1464884920968440

Newsom, D. A., Carrell, B., & Hussain, S. (1992). *The tower of babel: A descriptive report on attitudes toward the idea of integrated communication programs.* Association for Education in Journalism and Mass Communication.

Nixon, S. (2003). *Advertising cultures.* SAGE.

Patrutiu, L. (2015). Content marketing-the fundamental tool of digital marketing. *Bulletin of the Transilvania University of Brasov. Economic Sciences. Series V. 8, 57*(2), 111–118.

Pavlou, P. A., & Stewart, D. W. (2000). Measuring the effects and effectiveness of interactive advertising: A research agenda. *Journal of Interactive Advertising, 1*(1), 61–77. https://doi.org/10.1080/15252019.2000.10722044

Peláez, B. (2020, December 10). Las opiniones online generan un alto nivel de confianza y son clave en el proceso de compra. *Capterra.* https://www.capterra.es/blog/1847/opiniones-online-generan-confianza-son-clave-proceso-compra

Pfau, M., & Wan, H.-H. (2006). Persuasion: An intrinsic function of public relations. In C. H. Botan & V. Hazleton (Eds.), *Public relations theory II* (pp. 101–136). Lawrence Erlbaum Associates Publishers.

Potts, J. (2011). *Creative industries and economic evolution.* Edward Elgar Publishing.

PRovoke & NowGoCreate. (2021). Creativity in PR 2021 global study. *PRovoke.* www.provokemedia.com/ranking-and-data/creativity-in-pr

Richards, J. I., & Curran, C. M. (2002). Oracles on "advertising": Searching for a definition. *Journal of Advertising, 31*(2), 63–77. https://doi.org/10.1080/009133 67.2002.10673667

Rose, P. B. (1996). Practitioner opinions and interests regarding integrated marketing communications in selected Latin American countries. Journal of Marketing Communications, 2(3), 125–139.

Samuel, L. R. (2012). Thinking smaller: Bill Bernbach and the creative revolution in advertising of the 1950s. *Advertising & Society Review*, 13(3).

Sánchez-Guijaldo, M. P. (2017). Periodismo ciudadano, ¿un nuevo fenómeno de periodismo? *Documentación de las Ciencias de la Información, 40*, 31–54. http://dx.doi.org/10.5209/DCIN.57161

Santora, J. (2022, March 29). Key influencer marketing statistics you need to know for 2022. *Influencer Marketing Hub.* https://influencermarketinghub.com/influencer-marketing-statistics/

Schultz, D. E., Tannenbaum, S. I., & Lauterborn, R. F. (1993). Integrated marketing communications. NTC Business Books.

Schultz, M., & Ervolder, L. (1998). Culture, identity and image consultancy: Crossing boundaries between management, advertising, public relations and design. *Corporate Reputation Review, 2*(1), 29–50.

Seran (Potra), S., & Izvercian, M. (2014). Prosumer engagement in innovation strategies: The prosumer creativity and focus model. *Management Decision, 52*(10), 1968–1980. https://doi.org/10.1108/MD-06-2013-0347

Sgarbossa, F. (n.d.). La identidad visual como puente entre Diseño Gráfico y RRPP. *Foro Alfa.* https://foroalfa.org/articulos/la-identidad-visual-como-puente-entre-diseno-grafico-y-rrpp

Smith, R. D. (2013). *Strategic planning for public relations*. Routledge.

Sriramesh, K. (2010). Globalization and public relations. Opportunities for Growth and Reformulation. In Robert L. Heath (Ed.) *The SAGE Handbook of Public Relations* (pp. 691–707). London: SAGE.

Statista (2021, September 27). Influencer marketing worldwide – statistics & facts. *Statista*. www.statista.com/topics/2496/influence-marketing/#dossierKeyfigures

Suárez, J. C. (2017). El periodismo ciudadano. Análisis de opiniones de periodistas profesionales de España, Italia y Bélgica. *Convergencia, 24*(74), 91–111. https://doi.org/10.29101/crcs.v0i74.4383.

Sudhaman, A. (2021a, June 25). CEOs at cannes condensed: PR industry must 'wake up' to opportunity on offer. *PRovoke*. www.provokemedia.com/long-reads/article/ceos-at-cannes-condensed-pr-industry-must-'wake-up'-to-opportunity-on-offer

Sudhaman, A. (2021b, June 28). Creativity in PR Study: Talent, triggers & techniques in the lockdown era. *PRovoke*. www.provokemedia.com/long-reads/article/creativity-in-pr-study-talent-triggers-techniques-in-the-lockdown-era

Tamble, M. (2019, February 20). 7 tips for using visual content marketing. *Social Media Today*. www.socialmediatoday.com/news/7-tips-for-using-visual-content-marketing/548660/

Taylor, M. (2000). Cultural variance as a challenge to global public relations: A case study of the Coca-Cola scare in Europe. *Public Relations Review, 26*(3), 277–293. https://doi.org/10.1016/S0363-8111(00)00048-5

Tenderich, B., & Williams, J. (2014). *Transmedia branding*. Eimo.

The Holmes Report & NowGoCreate (2013). *Creativity in PR. A global study*. https://es.slideshare.net/ArunSudhaman/creativity-in-pr2013

Toffler, A. (1980). *The third wave*. Pan Books.

USC Annenberg Center for Public Relations (2021) *2021 Global Communications Report*. Los Angeles, California, April 2021. https://assets.uscannenberg.org/docs/cpr-2021-gcr.pdf

Wakefield, R. I. (2010). Why Culture Is Still Essential in Discussions About Global Public Relation. In Heath, R. L. (Ed.) *The SAGE Handbook of Public Relations* (pp. 659–670). Sage.

Witkowski, T. H. (2008). Antiglobal challenges to marketing in developing countries. In M. Tadajewski & D. Brownlie (Eds.), *Critical marketing: Issues in contemporary marketing* (pp. 211–244). Wiley & Sons.

Xifra, J. (2014). *Manual de Relaciones Públicas e Institucionales*. Tecnos.

Zerfass, A., Vercic, D., & Wiesenberg, M. (2016). The dawn of a new golden age for media relations? How PR professionals interact with the mass media and use new collaboration practices. *Public Relations Review, 42*(4), 499–508.

Zoch, L. M., Supa, D. W., & VanTuyll, D. R. (2014). The portrayal of public relations in the era of Ivy Lee through the lens of the New York Times. *Public Relations Review, 40*(4), 723–732.

5 Conclusion

PR is a creative industry that continually adapts to changing circumstances. Throughout its history, it has had to adapt to social and cultural changes, and today, it is particularly affected by the globalization of the economy and technological advances. Nonetheless, tackling these challenges presents tremendous opportunities, as they allow reaching wider audiences, while at the same time establishing a more personal connection with them.

Creativity has long been recognized as one of the key competencies of a PR practitioner, but its place within the industry has only begun to be studied in recent years. In contrast, other disciplines such as Psychology have spent decades defining creativity and studying how it can be stimulated at the individual and organizational level. Thus, the nondeterministic theories defined creativity as a skill that can be stimulated and pointed out the importance of the interaction between the individual and the environment. Flexibility, originality, and fluidity are among the concepts derived from psychology as components of creativity.

According to this rationale, creativity in PR is understood as the ability to generate new, unique, and appropriate ideas that allow organizations to solve their communication problems.

PR is defined as a strategic process designed to help organizations establish and maintain mutually beneficial relationships with their audiences. Hence, creativity must be applied to achieve this objective and the proposals resulting from this process must be aligned with the mission, vision, and values of the organization.

The PR industry caters to a wide range of organizations and entities, including private individuals, celebrities, large corporations, small and medium-sized companies, nonprofit organizations, NGOs, political parties, governments, activist groups, and organized social movements. In this way, PR and creativity transcend being only about serving organizations, but can be viewed from a global perspective, focusing on how they contribute to society. In other words, PR can contribute to achieving UN SDGs and the

DOI: 10.4324/9781003246879-5

2030 Agenda by raising public awareness and changing citizens' behavior on such issues as climate change, gender equality, and social rights.

Additionally, the PR field has many specializations, ranging from media relations, event management, and internal communication to lobbying, public affairs, and CSR. Similarly, the techniques and tactics that can be adopted in PR are wide-ranging and diverse, and each can benefit from the adoption of creativity.

The PR industry is made up by PR consultancies, from full-service agencies to creative boutiques, in-house communication departments, and freelance professionals. Women make up most of the industry, but they still represent a small minority in management positions.

In PR, creativity cannot be regarded simply as an individual quality, but rather from a collaborative perspective, in which the different professionals involved in the design and execution of communication plans work together as a team. Therefore, creativity is also an organizational competence and an asset that grows from combining the knowledge of the members of the group, while at the same time it must be stimulated by the organization itself and its managers.

In addition, creativity should be applied throughout the entire PR process, that is, not only in the formulation of the message or the format of the actions, but at every stage, including research, planning, execution, and evaluation of a campaign.

In fact, creativity has come to be considered an essential element for successful PR. It is therefore essential to understand how we can encourage creativity within the sector. Many techniques can be used to achieve this. However, few of them are known within the sector. One of the most common methods is brainstorming, which is frequently not even done properly. Among other techniques that can be implemented are brainwriting, the 635 method, SCAMPER, Six Thinking Hats, mind mapping, provocative operation (PO), synectics, and attribute listing. As each of these techniques is directed toward enhancing fluency, flexibility, originality, elaboration, sensitivity, and/or redefinition, in response to communication challenges or opportunities, it may be better to apply one or the other depending on the creative need in each case.

In order to enhance creativity in the PR industry, it is also proposed to (1) encourage management to foster trust so that PR practitioners can express ideas freely, work autonomously, and have the necessary economic resources and time to do their jobs; (2) take risks and tolerate the ambiguity which often comes with the process of creative thinking; (3) combat negativity, identifying and removing barriers to creativity; (4) incorporate the role of creative director, that is, someone who can lead teams in developing creative concepts, offer creative guidance, know how to apply creative techniques, evaluate creative ideas, and defend proposed creative solutions to decision makers; (5) create an environment that encourages creativity by making organizational changes and changes in work routines such as mixing members from different teams who may have not worked together previously; (6) avoid the risks caused by hyper-specialization, both in terms of sectors and PR techniques; (7) train in creative skills, for example by consulting specialized resources, hosting workshops, analyzing success stories, etc.; (8)—as indicated earlier—apply creativity techniques beyond brainstorming; (9) value diversity at all levels, including mixing practitioners with different creativity-related skills (members with stronger fluency, originality, flexibility, or production abilities); (10) encourage motivation, both extrinsic (through remuneration or rewards) and intrinsic (by giving team members stimulating tasks based on their preferences).

All this in a world that is increasingly connected and full of communication content, where the audiences with whom organizations wish to communicate and establish relationships are becoming increasingly saturated and PR needs to find ways to attract their attention. For this purpose, some trends identified in PR are as follows. (1) The importance of appealing to audiences' emotions when developing communication campaigns, especially when the audiences are saturated with informative content and struggle to respond to rational arguments. (2) The use of storytelling, that has always been part of PR, but nowadays it is extremely useful when it comes to telling stories related to organizations, often in transmedia formats. (3) Digitalization and, derived from it, the importance of audiovisual formats when it comes to developing content and building relationships with social media users. (4) The rise of podcasts, which can be informative, educational, and entertaining and can help organizations connect with their stakeholders in more meaningful ways. (5) Virtual and hybrid events, which are more sustainable, cost-effective, customized, and accessible and do not require participants to travel. While the live experience is still a powerful factor in terms of impact on key audiences, in the future, efforts will be made to enhance the experience in digital environments, for example in shared virtual spaces such as the metaverse. (6) Adapting to COVID-19 and learning the lesson in order to prepare for future epidemiological crises or global climate catastrophes. In the midst of the pandemic, many challenges arose, but there were also opportunities, such as the increased demand for crisis and risk communication services; the need for internal communication to maintain a sense of belonging, despite physical distancing, among organizations' employees; the importance of CSR, which demonstrates that society expects organizations to contribute to its well-being, and the value of creativity in finding solutions to communication problems as they arise. (7) The value of internal communication, which has gone beyond responding to the exceptional situation caused by the pandemic and has become an integral part of corporate communication plans in recent years. (8) The need for organizations to have a purpose, a mission, a vision, and values that they can share with their audiences; as well as a rise in CSR and the need for organizations to be accountable to society for their impact on the environment and the population.

Finally, we must not forget that PR work alongside other creative industries, including marketing, advertising, journalism, and graphic design. In all of them, creativity plays a fundamental role, and even more so in the current scenario where there is a convergence of communication practices in the digital environment, such as brand journalism, UGC, influencer relations, native advertising, advertiser funded media content, branded content, content marketing or sponsored content, among others, that emphasizes the importance of developing creative, original, and innovative content capable of attracting the attention of organizations' key audiences. This leads, at the same time, to disciplinary reflections on these new techniques, which are often hybrid in nature. In any case, PR professionals must be able to collaborate with those of other creative industries, while applying the ethical principles of their own profession, since, although creativity offers unconventional solutions to communication problems, these solutions must always adhere to professional ethics and existing codes of ethics—most of which are drafted by the professional associations themselves.

Index

Note: Page numbers in **bold** indicate a box or table on the corresponding page.

Printed in the United States
by Baker & Taylor Publisher Services

Printed in the United States
by Baker & Taylor Publisher Services